CW00692475

FUN, FLIES AND LAUGHTER
– A Stirling Life

John Gilbert

ARTHUR H. STOCKWELL LTD.
Torrs Park   Ilfracombe   Devon
Established 1898
www.ahstockwell.co.uk

First published in Great Britain, 2006

British Library Cataloguing-in-Publication Data.
A catalogue record for this book is available
from the British Library.

Arthur H. Stockwell Ltd. bears no responsibility
for the accuracy of events recorded in this book.

The author wishes to acknowledge that the poems and odes referred to may be subject to an undisclosed copyright. Notwithstanding, prior to publication, although unsuccessful, the author has made every possible effort to trace the writers, their families or representatives in order to seek their kind permission. If notified, the publisher will be pleased to rectify any errors or omissions at the earliest opportunity.

The Author

John H. C. Gilbert was born in 1946. He was educated at Rydens Secondary Modern School, Walton-on-Thames, Surrey, and served almost thirty years in the Surrey Police, attaining the rank of Inspector. From his home in the Surrey village of Ripley, situated only one mile from the R.H.S. Gardens at Wisley, he now writes about Canada's participation in the Battle for Normandy. The son of a French Canadian tank gunner, his specialised topic is the fierce and often brutal fighting to liberate Caen, Field Marshal Montgomery's most treasured D-Day objective!

By the same Author:
 Bloody Buron! Canada's D-Day + 1
 Only Death Could Land. The Canadian Attack on Carpiquet, July 1944
 www.canadasnormandywarbooks.com

ISBN 0-7223-3786-8
ISBN 978-0-7223-3786-8
*Printed in Great Britain by
Arthur H. Stockwell Ltd.
Torrs Park   Ilfracombe
Devon*

Dedication

In memory of my father-in-law and friend,
Henry Hay Dundas Stirling, BA, a fisherman.
(b.3 July 1919, Simla, India.)
AND
To the Tobs!

THE FISHERMAN'S PRAYER

Lord suffer me to catch a fish
So large that even I
In talking of it afterward
Shall have no need to lie.

Henry and Fifi – with the first fish of 1976.

TO A TROUT

by Oliver St John Gogarty

Into the brilliant air you leap,
Leaving your dim immortal home.
Quick as a thought out of the deep
Into a living word may come.
Why do you leave the lonely gloom
Whose floors are paved, when waves are sunny,
With golden patinas on the brown
All pleasanter than last year's honey?

Not where the winds and waters make
A miracle of purple wine,
Nor where the margin of the brake
Is sanded to a crescent line,
And hollies for a moment shine
Like Thyades when they're undressing;
But where the floating lily isles
Have kept the ripples from transgressing.

None knows what makes you spring in air;
And no one knows what sets me silly,
Why with a hookless bait I fare,
A hookless fly and dumb gillie,
To cast for Beauty on the wind.
While tempting Fate's your like employment;
Then why should Life bewail its end,
If Death's the salt of all enjoyment?

Table of Contents

Acknowledgements

According to the author and great cricket enthusiast Sir Pelham Warner, the charismatic and dynamic orator, Winston Spencer Churchill, in his speech at the *Sunday Times* Book Exhibition during the autumn of 1949 spoke of the "adventure" of writing a book:

'To begin with, it is a toy and an amusement; then it becomes a mistress, and then it becomes a master, and then a tyrant. The last phase is that just as you are about to be reconciled to your servitude, you kill the monster, and fling him out to the public.'

In writing *Fun, Flies and Laughter,* my third book, I have been through all these phases in almost equal measure. However, in considering my enthusiasm and genuine warmth for Henry Hay Dundas Stirling, my father-in-law, and the worthy traditions and magical experiences of his era, a period very much enhanced from his dramatic appearance, some additional words of Sir Pelham come to mind: Respect carried me through at moments when I felt like falling by the wayside.

I am extremely fortunate to have acquired quite unreservedly the full support of Henry's immediate and extended family, in particular my lovely sister-in-law Jenny. Mirroring my fond memories of his colourful and boisterous character, they without question also admired the immense sense of fun and laughter that Henry (Pa Tob) brought to each and every one of their respective lives. Belated thanks must also be generously given to Betty (Ma Tob), a truly remarkable character in her own right. Throughout her marriage to the untroubled Henry, she carefully and painstakingly gathered a most interesting portfolio of photographs, letters, diplomas, certificates and newspaper cuttings. Her passion for romantic nostalgia, however, was not an addiction to the hoarding of clutter, but originated from a genuine love of the arts, including theatre and the comparatively modern phenomenon of the cinema. At this point, I should also add that looking through her meticulously detailed scrapbook was a complete and memorable joy, especially browsing through cut-out illustrations of 'Golden Era' celebrities: Joan Crawford and Clark Gable, Jeanette MacDonald, Anita Louise and Paul Muni. And who, over a certain magical age, could possibly forget: Chaplin, Cary Grant, Bing Crosby and Frances Drake, Mae West and Jack Buchanan, Ginger Rogers and Fred Astaire along with their contemporaries, Garbo, Douglas Fairbanks Junior, Spencer Tracy, Judy Garland and a host of others too numerous to mention? It was, therefore, Betty's sheer determination to retain the pleasures from her past, together with her natural flair for astonishing foresight that has made this book possible.

In spite of such a wealth of wonderful material, I could not have contemplated or actually embarked upon such an enormous endeavour without the understanding and most loyal support so freely given by my beautiful wife Fiona. Throughout the process of researching Henry's most fascinating life, she was to endure several arduous rail journeys in India. Even more demanding, was that during these particularly tiresome exploits she was usually feeling under the weather, not only owing to fatigue but also owing to an acute bout of what is now internationally acclaimed as being the infamous *Delhi belly*! However, in spite of this rather common albeit exacting problem, in common with her remarkable father, she seems to have inherited the blessing of becoming even more delightful in spirit and youthful in looks as years tend to gather pace.

Thanks also to the lovely Jeannie Stirrup, our travelling companion. A close friend of Fiona's since the seventies, Jeannie is a photographic genius. And thanks to Jeannie's husband, our mutual friend Mike. Without his kind and thoughtful approval, Jeannie's help would have been very sorely missed.

On a similar theme, I am also grateful to the author T. C. Ivens, who wrote the outstanding *Still Water Fly-Fishing*, and to Macmillan Publishing, London. Without the assistance of Caroline Glover, who kindly granted copyright permission, my book would be totally void of those excellent illustrations depicting the art and immense skill of casting.

Similarly, many thanks to Solo Syndication/Associated Newspapers, especially Rebecca Barnard, for allowing the publication of those amazing newspaper cuttings that illustrate the dogged Detective Inspector Grove, Henry's lookalike, and his illustrious companion Paul Temple, the famous television sleuth.

A word of thanks must also be given to the following friends of the family, who in their own unique way have helped to corroborate my deeply felt admiration for Henry Hay Dundas: to a most delightful quartet of ladies, Mary McNamara, Cora Portillo, Betty's sister Margaret Winkley and Betty's childhood friend, Lady Sheila Trevaskis; to the redoubtable Peter Paine, CBE, who added Henry's style of banter to wonderfully detailed anecdotal evidence; to Betty Buchanan, a most adventurous globetrotter, whose well-known passion for travel led her to Gargunnock House, and whose vivid recollection of the visit helps portray the true splendour of the prodigious estate; to Mary and Dominic McDonnell; to Graham and Shirley Palmer; and to Dympna Ambrose, wife of the caring and compassionate Dr Geoffrey Ambrose, who, up until the very end, displayed what true friendship really entails.

On a much lighter note, thanks also to the two 'best tree surgeons in Christendom', the incredibly well-informed James (Jim) Bilston and his old friend Alfie, now sadly departed. Jim's enchanting stories of their frequent visits to Moor Cottage will be for ever cherished.

Very much in a similar vein, I am also extremely grateful to Commodore A. K. Darwish, head of military at the Egyptian Embassy, London. Although unable to help a great deal, his masterful understanding of British humour, especially relating to Egyptian record-keeping, was quite incredible. This was particularly true of his joking over the telephone, and, above all, his candid explanation of how during the Second World War young and injured British soldiers frequently bonded in adversity with even younger and usually much fitter Egyptian nurses!

Further thanks must be given to Retha Louw, a reception-administrator at the Deciduous Fruit Producers' Trust, Cape Town (formerly the Deciduous Fruit Board), whose knowledge of earlier times and of past employees was invaluable; and to Julie Rose, a friend of the outspoken Geoffrey Boycott, and PA to the director of the splendid Mount Nelson Hotel, also located in Cape Town. Her kindness and help was truly appreciated. The partaking of morning coffee, while rummaging through several boxes of Union-

Castle Line memorabilia, remains to this day quite unforgettable. On this point thanks must also be bestowed upon my friend Richard Johnston, an ex-employee of this once famous shipping company. To browse though and research his vast collection of *Clansman* (*British & Commonwealth Review*) magazines was a delight and most helpful.

Thanks also to the amiable yet rather shy parish priest of St Michael's Church, Shimla, Father Xavier Holland. His marvellously calm and genteel hospitality was most welcome. Additional thanks must pass to Xavier's extremely busy housekeeper, who, in keeping with most parish helpers, displayed a hugely contrasting, particularly jaunty air of pride in her auspicious position by gleefully preparing tea.

More thanks should be given to the archivists of Downside School, Peterhouse College, Cambridge and St Catherine's College, Oxford – Father Phillips, Margaret Davies and Dr Philip Pattenden respectively. Their meticulous searches helped to resurrect, and in many instances confirm, Henry's academic achievements. Another archives helper deserving a word of thanks is Linda Nelson, administrations officer at the Army Personnel Centre, Glasgow.

It would be amiss of me not to also mention two other close friends, Derek Fieldman and Derek Denby. For several years both have endured the pain of having a temperamental writer as a friend, especially a friend who has become a writing anorak and, as far as IT and the digital revolution is concerned, an acute technophobe.

Last, but by no means least, many thanks must be given to Peter Nicholas and Richard Stockwell, directors of Arthur H. Stockwell Ltd. (book publishers since 1898). Once again, without their kindness and help the book will still have remained a pipe dream.

Father Xavier Holland with Henry's youngest daughter, Fiona.

Introduction

There is no doubt that the second quarter of the 20th century was able to call upon some masterful personalities – Churchill, Mountbatten, the Kennedys and more. But there was one other extraordinary and paradoxical character, who, although not in any way ultra-patriotic like many ardent contemporaries, still managed to burst his way onto the global and international arena, bringing with him a curious amalgam of *Fun, Flies and Laughter* – Henry Hay Dundas Stirling, a direct descendant of the Feudal Barony of Gargunnock, Stirlingshire, Scotland. (*Crest:* a Saracen's head enwreathed proper. *Motto*: Gang forward)

Comprehensively and deeply researched, this biography charts his colourful life, which included a privileged upbringing, successful education and several amusing achievements.

Having chronicled his early years spent fishing and shooting in and around Simla (now Shimla, in the northern province of Himachal Pradesh) in British Imperial India, *Fun, Flies and Laughter* traces Henry's initial education at Downside School and Peterhouse College, Cambridge, before the Second World War rudely interrupted his future plans of married bliss and joie de vivre!

The story traces how despite being the only child born to an eminent Scottish engineer (James Hay Stirling, b.12 March 1882 at Gargunnock House) and a highly respected Irish Republican physician (Blanche Gertrude Columba Griffin, daughter of Dr Thomas Griffin) he enthusiastically placed his education on hold by taking up a commission as 2nd lieutenant, Royal Artillery. Thereafter the narrative explains how having been severely wounded while serving in North Africa and after spending a year in a Cairo hospital, family influence and "the pulling of apron strings" led Henry to the relative safety of Kashmir. The incongruities of his dutiful acquiescence to the whims of an overprotective mother is identified by the forlorn Henry, much to the chagrin of his lonely bride back in Blitz-torn London. He *reluctantly* agreed to convalesce the rest of the conflict in the serene panoramic foothills of the Himalayas, sandwiched between the Punjab and Tibet. Once settled, his physiotherapy programme, so painstakingly drafted by his mother, would be harsh. He would focus his mind away from dangerous gallantry and tackle duties more in keeping with his true status. Along with study he should ride, shoot and fish with impunity!

Noting that the early post-war years brought a welcomed reuniting with his love and an Oxford honours degree in botanical forestry, *Fun, Flies and Laughter* also studies one of the mysteries of attaining an Oxbridge education – the progression of the intellectual academics into the relatively unrelated domain of the 'cut and thrust' business sector. Henry's sterling vitality and pragmatic and outspoken opinions, together with a keen passion for a sybaritic lifestyle (that included of course the artistic joy of fly-fishing while munching smoked salmon sandwiches made in the Irish way), shines through the account of his working years both in Garrick Street, WC2 and St George's Street, Cape Town, South Africa with the Deciduous Fruit Board. Indeed, well before failing heath, the cause of early retirement during 1977, the gregarious Henry not only managed to outwit the celebrity panel of *What's My Line?* by casting his amusing parody as a peach-taster, but also gained further notoriety by giving approval to his craggy, firm-chinned and aristocratic profile being imitated to characterise the steadfast Detective Inspector Grove in Francis Durbridge's serialisation of *Paul Temple*.

In addition – and so typical of the gifted and courageous man who with gritty determination continually battled against the uncertainties of a serious heart condition – nothing would please him more than partying. He enjoyed homely gatherings, where not only a social drink, good food and interesting company was the order of the day, and also occasions where fervent and sometimes fiery parleys abounded. These numerous sojourns were venues of absolute delight for the mischievous Henry, who would frequently add wit, provocation and acute sharpness to debate, deliberately portraying an amusing yet belligerent role as devil's advocate during the many discussions on politics, world affairs and, inevitably, the skills of fishing!

The narrative also reveals a contrasting almost paradoxical side of Henry, who as keen listener and agreeable counsellor, particularly in the calm serenity of his home and family, was unusually shy and courteous. He utilised gentler, more oblique methods of making his views known and, more often than not, they were graciously accepted. Finally, as the biography unfolds it describes how with the aid of youthful looks, and a warm smile, the rebellious, convivial Henry Hay Dundas Stirling with his haughty, penetrating laugh cheerfully ignored nagging ill health and disagreeable companionship and readily embraced an untroubled philosophy of *Carpe Diem* – living for today. With an understanding that happiness heals and that smiling and laughing are both powerful accessories to more conventional medicine, Henry's larger-than-life and exceptionally positive attitude was especially noticeable whilst in the company of his innumerable and wide-ranging friends, amongst whom was a former confidant and neighbour in Stanmore – Luis Gabriel Portillo, a Spanish Castilian refugee and father of the charismatic Michael.

In short, *Fun, Flies and Laughter – A Stirling Life* is a litany of treasured anecdotal memoirs, fishing records and a collection of wonderful keepsakes. Woven together, they expose how upon a truly international stage a talented fisherman and a gifted friend captivated not only sea trout and salmon, but also everyone who was privileged to have shared his companionship. Each reveal one common purpose: to interpret the thoughts of a most remarkable and generous maverick, a fortuitous rebel who revelled in an era now past where conflict and adversity was successfully tempered by wholesome fun, a worthy recreation and honest laughter – a period that very many today would still argue was "The Golden Age" of the 20th century.

The entrance to St Michael's Cathedral, Shimla.
Darwaje Ke Pichae Azad Zindagi – Beyond these doors lies a sterling life.

CHAPTER ONE

Pruning the Family Tree

ACT I

'The British had discovered the spot (Shimla) in the 1820s, and it was so much to their liking that in 1864 it was declared their summer capital. At that time one fifth of the human race was administered from Shimla.'

Raaja Bhasin, author

Henry Hay Dundas Stirling, BSc, was an enigma, an *enfant* of many worlds: the quarrelsome old world of Great Britain and Europe; the brash and increasingly manipulative new world across the mighty Atlantic (two disagreeable features that were not lost on Henry, who never made a crossing); and finally the vast world of British Imperial India with its hugely divergent lifestyles.

Even more confounding was that the colonial and paradoxical Henry, without having inherited one trace of Anglo-Saxon blood, was the classical epitome of an English country gentleman! Such was the strength of his Anglophile thoughts and deeds that for Henry, like "most of the English, their history is just that, history".[1] There was not any lingering hint of intense Celtic patriotism, so ably narrated by Jeremy Paxman in his humorous book on *The English* where he suggests that in both Scotland and Ireland "Every self-respecting adult considers themselves to belong to an unbroken tradition stretching back to the wearing of woad; oppressed peoples remember their history." [2] In spite of Henry's particularly laconic views upon his Celtic roots, there is little doubt that during his later years his colourful and interesting multi-heritage, together with a powerful and deeply felt passion for calm undisturbed natural beauty and contrasting boisterous joie de vivre, were all extremely recognisable and were immensely significant. The unusual accumulation would not only influence his passion for Scottish smoked salmon upon Irish soda bread but would provide the catalyst of his unyielding views upon world order and his deeply felt Catholic faith, inasmuch as every one of God's subjects has a unique intrinsic raison d'etre. Perhaps of equal consequence, Henry was resolute in his opinion that as meagre humans we should all take stock and strive to respect one another in spite of class, colour or creed, as well as protecting our wonderful yet highly fragile environment. Indeed, his love of the wilderness, particularly hills, woodland and lakes, was such that they amounted to more than just tranquil havens but venues where he could escape from the inevitable demands and drama of everyday life. It was the sheer joy of being totally immersed within such scenic splendour and the calm, pleasurable yet occasionally challenging pastime of fly-fishing, particularly deep in the unspoilt countryside of Ireland, that thoroughly convinced him that everyone without exception should be taught the sport. Pragmatically, he hoped that through an appreciation of fly-fishing people would come to reflect upon the life-giving wonder of photosynthesis and to understand the folly of uncontrolled deforestation.

Henry was born on 3 July 1919 in Simla, India, the old capital of the Punjab, now called Shimla, in the northern province of Himachal Pradesh – a beautifully cultured European retreat set high in the Shivalik foothills. He had innocently entered a most bewitching and beautiful country adorned by palaces and riches of the past for the privileged few. Yet, at the same time, it was a huge unbending nation touched by the crippling poverty of the vast majority, with many city-dwellers sleeping in the filthy mosquito-riddled ditches that straddle dirt roads and cart tracks. None of this unsavoury squalor, however, was bestowed upon the fortunate Henry. He had come into an advantaged family that enjoyed a social calendar of gaieties and frivolities within the very hub of the thriving Simla society. An example of just how terribly prestigious Simla had become during that awesome period of British colonial rule is that for the six months of summer the hill station not only became the centre of operations of the civil and military government of Britannia's India but also hosted the central headquarters of the King-Emperor's Empire.

Whereas today the picturesque hill town that also governed British

Kashmir has very little administrative importance, it can still provide a stunning gateway to the world's most famous backdrop – the mountain range of the mighty Himalayas. Even now, with overseas travel becoming commonplace, to very many British subjects the Himalayas, a mass of unbroken rock stretching 1,800 miles that umbrellas the vastness of the Indian subcontinent, undeniably stirs memories of their younger more scholarly days. In that period, most primary and secondary schools, as well as grammars and universities that provided the backcloth to the old British establishment, were unashamedly and rather jingoistically patriotic, clinging unknowingly yet hopelessly to British imperialism across the forever diminishing globe. The true heroes of that era who were nominated as House or group names for inter-school activities were not the likes of the much admired N. W. D. Yardley, a *Gentleman* cricketer, or *Players* of the great game in the mould of Len Hutton and Denis Compton. In the late forties and early fifties pulses raced in response to newsreels showing the gallant exploits of courageous explorers and brave adventurers. Men such as these were our national icons, and none more so than the New Zealand-born mountaineer and explorer Sir Edmund Hillary, who coincidentally shared the same year and month of birth as Henry.

With modern technology and endless resources now readily available to amateur and professional researchers alike, there have been numerous television programmes that have perhaps superseded the steadfast achievements of Hillary and his equally courageous and loyal companion, the tireless Sherpa Tenzing. Even before the digital revolution, excellent automated cameras have been able to supply to our living rooms truly splendid bird's-eye views of the range that includes Mount Everest, the highest peak on earth.

Amazing as it may seem, it was this superlative setting, still occasionally described by English-speaking guides as "Cheltenham in India", that was to smile upon and warmly greet the baby Henry, after he had first gently rubbed and focused his tender eyes toward a doting mother and a new beginning. And what a beginning! His mother had numerous beneficial connections in very high places, particularly in Jodhpur, and she unashamedly adored riding and shooting. His father held a prominent appointment with the country's Northern Railways Board, and he similarly loved riding, shooting game and above all else fishing. His eminence in the equestrian community meant that, in common with the military, especially well-connected young subalterns of cavalry, he enjoyed the delight

A Stirling base camp set high in the Shivalik Hills part of the mighty Himalayas.

The Stirling family home in Shimla.

of having a handicap in the sport that Churchill once described as "your passport to the world" – the breathtaking game of polo. Furthermore, an old and much treasured photograph tends to suggest that, bearing in mind his parents' positions, sometime during Henry's introduction to the sport he had also watched his father play the wonderful game alongside the very great Raja Hanut Singh – probably the most famous player of all time. Incidentally the name polo is British, a derivative of the Balti word for ball, while the game itself has its origins in the Balistan region of the Western Himalayas.

Destined to be an only child, Henry was nevertheless able to call upon a large extended family of local shikaris (beaters), guides and stable coolies (assistants) together with several horses and hill ponies, and domestic pets that included numerous game retrievers and spaniels. More wondrous was that these privileges and infinitely expensive outdoor pursuits were blessed opportunities, enhanced by a magnificent home that nestled comfortably within the Himalayan foothills. Even more astonishing was that the household could still rely upon an assortment of British provisions that had been at first dispatched by sea, then by rail, before being transported by ekkas (wooden carts) drawn by local ghoonts (hill ponies). Several loyal and dedicated servants were at hand in order to keep the family home in pristine condition.

Unquestionably, one of Henry's most obvious influences was the quirkiness of his adoring mother, Blanche Gertrude Columba Stirling, BCh, MB, née Griffin (b.1887, Dublin; educated at University College Dublin), the daughter of Dr Thomas Griffin. Although an accomplished Irish physician, surgeon and obstetrician in her own right, and in spite of an extremely fortunate upbringing in the close proximity of a vibrant and cultured Dublin, it would be a gross distortion of the truth to say that Blanche was a great lover of Imperial Britain, particularly of the English! Her family ties and loyalties during a tremendously difficult period of Anglo-Irish history could at best be described as principally colourful, and at worst as somewhat subversive. Although undeniably advantaged, her time at University College Dublin had stirred a rebellious streak that would remain with her throughout an adventurous medical career and later motherhood. As a supporter of Republicanism and its quest for unfettered control of the country, in accordance with the seditious Proclamation of 1916, Blanche, who had lived and studied in Dublin during the rise of the Irish Socialist Republican Party, was it seems particularly scathing of the dominated English. Encouraged by the slogan-shouting

A side elevation of the Stirling family home – note the Himalayan backcloth and a loyal servant posing as footman/guard.

Raj Hanut Singh – probably the world's most famous polo player.

followers of the party's founder, the revolutionary James Connolly, Blanche would have no doubt echoed his utter contempt for Britain and agreed with his argument that the development of democracy in Ireland had been smothered by an ungodly Union. Another noted and interesting aside to her early days and of her deeply held political persuasions was that her journalist brother, Gerald, wrote (for its time) a highly controversial novel. *The Dead March Past* was a semi-autographical saga that depicted the curious and indecisive life of a County Mayo tinker, who loathed politics and politicians, and felt aggrieved by Law. With chapters entitled *The Tinker "Stafes" the Huns, The Tinker and the Provost of Trinity*, and *The Tinker, the Tan and the Poet*, the contentious narrative acclaims how the actions of the ghost-like innocent who was forever seeking justice for a wrongly accused ancestor, subsequently troubled and infuriated both De Valera's Home Rule supporters and London's paramilitary mercenaries, the notorious Black and Tans.

Indeed, so great were some of the criticisms of its publication that the dismayed author felt it necessary to write a column in the *Irish Independent* rebutting claims of having possible Fenian allegiances abroad and any homeland alignment to the subversive Irish Republicans. The article suitably emphasised to the readership that the novel contained the poignant passage *"Is Fairrige mor idir Eirann agus an Oileann nua"* (Gaelic – there is a big sea between Ireland and America), and that undaunted by others and their opinions he remained a committed pacifist who was passionately against conflict and any rearmament programme.

On a much lighter note, it was perhaps her brother's influence and ability with the pen that led her to her first love and ex-fiancé, Oliver St John Gogarty, a young friend of the renowned Irish poet William Butler Yeats. The handsome and dashing Gogarty, who like Blanche had pursued his father's profession, was also a budding rebel and talented medical student in the making. Indeed, following his degree, not only did he enjoy success as a highly qualified physician specialising in ear, nose and throat, but also as a gifted writer of plays and poetic prose. Perhaps his best-known work was his enchanting book *An Offering of Swans and Other Poems* which included *To a Trout* – a poem that Henry would have unquestionably enjoyed.

With this avant-garde, stylish yet staunchly independent backdrop to her informative years, and being a free-thinking and spirited modern woman, it was to make perfect sense that, should harmony

Blanche Gertrude Columba Stirling – a most remarkable woman.

Henry bonding with a doting mother.

be expected in any future relationship, a prospective husband would need qualities of intellect, calm, compassion, understanding and a great deal of dogged patience. James Hay Stirling, BSc (b.1882, Gargunnock; educated at King William's College, IOM, late State Railways Service, Jodhpur, and Rajputana), was such a man, in spite of being a Scottish Protestant! Although of remarkable complexity, it will serve little purpose to fully exhibit the complete lineage of Henry's father, the noble and dignified James Hay Stirling, yet it would be a grave injustice and a mistake to merely state that he was truly a kind and compassionate Scottish gentleman with a sharp methodical mind, who originated from a distinguished pedigree with known family lineage of decorous antecedents dating as far back as William the Conqueror. A limited précis can reveal a family origin that is completely entwined amongst the sturdy roots of Catholic Irish Celts, Scottish Picts and Protestant Saxons. The ancestors of Clan Buchanan Country, the 'home of the buck' (in old Saxon, *becca* or *bucca*, later *buccleugh*), with their battle cry of "Clar-Innis" (an island on Loch Lomond) "bore their full share of the military operations of their country" [3]

GENTLEMEN – THE TARTAN!

Here's to it!
The fighting sheen of it,
The yellow, the green of it,
The white, the blue of it,
The swing, the hue of it,
The dark, the red of it,
Every thread of it!
The fair have sighed for it,
The brave have died for it,
Heroes fought for it,
Foemen sought for it,
Honour the name of it,
Drink to the fame of it –
The Tartan! [4]

Within the clan's legacy, wrapped warmly in its bright intricate tartan made from wool from the mountains and dyes from the vale, and duly guarded by the motto *Clarior hinc honos* (Brighter hence the honour), are many notable clansmen – truly formidable characters such as William Buchanan of Auchmar; Anselan O'Kyan, the Fair, prince of Ulster; the Earl of Lennox; and a Highlander of more relevance, Sir William Stirling 1st of Keir, c.1420–1471. As an interesting aside, the ancient Clan Buchanan, septs and dependents (relatives from separate branches or 'broken men' – individuals seeking clan protection) can proudly claim to have included a former botanist, John Buchanan (1819–1898), who pursued a lifelong interest on the indigenous grasses of his adopted country, New Zealand.[5]

The ancient name of Stirling, a fortress from time immemorial, originates from a trilogy of primeval Celtic titles, Strvelyn, Striveling or Sturveling – meaning a place of strife. Overlooking the surrounding landscape, its lofty and dominating castle remains the principle feature of the especially intimidating stronghold and former royal residence of the Kings of Scotland cradled within its high walls. The formidable castle was the birthplace of James III, and possibly James IV, while its towering presence provided a fitting venue for the coronations of James V and of Mary. "The castle contains the *Parliament Hall*, built by James III; the *Palace* built by James V; and the *Chapel Royal*, rebuilt by James VI for the baptism of his son, Prince Henry."[6] From the castle, which predominately looks west over the lands of Buchanan, now Stirlingshire, "seven battlefields may be seen – including the scenes of the victories of Wallace and Bruce, Stirling Bridge (1297) and Bannockburn, near at hand".[7] To the east and across the Forth River are the ruins of the Cambuskenneth Abbey, founded by David I in for Augustinian canons. "Within its walls the Scottish Parliament was sat, and James III and his queen, Margaret of Denmark, were buried."[8] The nearby Wallace Monument at Causeway (220 feet high) not only commands a view only surpassed by that from the castle, but also acts as permanent reminder of the Battle of Stirling Bridge where 'Braveheart' William Wallace, determined to free the country from English domination, defeated the Anglo-Saxon army of King Edward.

To reiterate and complete Henry's (or *Eanruig* in Gaelic) earlier lineage, the union on his father's side with ancient European stock can be traced as far back as 1066 and King Harold's defeat at Hastings. Furthermore, an amusing genetic coincidence arises in that Henry and his father actually inherited William the Conqueror's crowning glory, a full head of auburn red hair – although, typical of Henry, he managed to retain his magnificent mane, *les cheveux châtains!*

A smiling Henry with a very proud father.

Like father, like son.

ACT II

'The ancient name of the parish of Gargunnock is Gargownno that was probably derived from the Celtic words Caer-guineach, a sharp or conical fortress.'

The Reverend James Laurie, minister

Having carefully yet somewhat cruelly pruned the Stirling family tree, Henry's lineage will commence in 1835, when Henry's great-grandfather Charles Stirling 1st of Gargunnock purchased Gargunnock House. Gargunnock House was built during the 15th and 16th centuries. The hall was remodelled around 1750, and the front altered and extended in 1789 in Adam style. There is a round original peel tower. It was bequeathed in 1989 to The Landmark Trust by Henry's cousin, Viola Henrietta Christian Stirling of Gargunnock, CBE (1948), TD (1951) and bars, FRHS, FSA Scot, of Gargunnock, Stirlingshire, Lady of the Feudal Barony of Gargunnock. (*Crest*: a Saracen's head enwreathed proper. *Motto*: Gang forward.)[9]

Gargunnock House is situated in the Forth Valley at the base of the Gargunnock Hills, which form part of the Lennox Range running from Stirling to Dumbarton, which extend through the southern breadth of the district. Gargunnock Parish has boundaries containing approximately 20 square miles. The highest point of these rolling hills is about 1,400 feet; and from their numerous summits there are fine views covering more than 12,000 square miles. The parish has a number of perennial springs, flowing from tilly or gravelly subsoils, resting on red and white sandstone rocks, which supplied the original inhabitants with an abundance of excellent water. The parish lands are still predominately moor, dryfield and carse. Most of the moor affords sound healthy pasture for sheep and cattle.[10]

During its illustrious past, Gargunnock House, which was very much cherished by Henry's proud cousin, entertained several prominent personalities. Among the most notable was the celebrated Polish composer and pianist Frederic Chopin. During his second visit to Scotland in 1848 he once played the home's pianoforte for his friend Jane Wilhelmina Stirling (1804–1859), Henry's great-great-aunt and a number of her selected guests.

More recently, however, during the darkest days of the Second World War, Prime Minister Churchill when on his frequent visits north would gratefully take up the offer to utilise its grand dining hall as a temporary War Cabinet office.

Gargunnock House.

'During one visit to Scotland when Henry was away fishing, Betty and I had tea at Gargunnock House with cousin Viola. I remember being very impressed with the piano, which Chopin had played, and the War Room where Churchill's War Cabinet met.'

Betty Buchanan, Kermarhin, France. 24 January 2006

Significantly and rather sadly, it appears that James Hay Stirling, Henry's father, was to be the last descendant to be born at Gargunnock House, the splendid centrepiece of the Stirling Feudal Barony.

It was not, though, a fortuitous bequest or a prodigious birthright, but a sense of adventure and a degree in mechanical engineering that subsequently enticed Henry's father to visit and for some while live and work in northern India. The capacity to be enthused by mathematics and his sound practical knowledge of natural science and the intricacies of physics, especially the complexities of its highly technical variants, matter and energy, were essential in the construction of secure and safe railway facilities in India, especially in the hazardous task of laying track upon difficult terrain.

There now lies a most mysterious episode: why did Henry's parents venture north to the Himalayan foothills? Whereas it is generally accepted that during the hot summer months many British ex-patriots followed the establishment's example of sensibly escaping the intense heat and humidity by moving to the cooler hill stations, there remains little evidence to support this claim. To some extent, though, there is one certainty: there was not a finer location more suited to a European lifestyle than British Kashmir, especially Simla. Looking at the dilemma logically, however, there were other more compelling arguments for Henry's father leaving the scorching plains of former Rajputana, now called Rajasthan. Blanche, his Catholic wife, was with child. Having successfully delivered his first-born, a baptism was urgently needed. This would be quickly followed by the requirement of a sound Catholic education. Again Simla, the home of the indigenous *vaivasis* (dwellers of hill forest), held the key to these logistical burdens, and, from a wonderful array of photographs of the period, it appears that the family stayed at Simla for some considerable time in spite of Blanche being the private physician to the Maharajah of Jodhpur, and Henry's father being the superintendent-in-charge of the district's expanding Bikaner Railway.

What is not in doubt is the immense pride that Henry's father would feel if only he were able to witness the hustle and bustle at the modern Jodhpur Railway Station – especially as the powerful

Bikaner–Howrah Express departs to Agra or the equally commanding Jaisalmer–Delhi Express leaves the city en route to the country's capital. And what would he now make of the midday event at Kalka Railway Station, when the comparatively modern express, aptly called the *Himalayan Queen*, arrives from its six-hour journey north from the crowded madness of the New Delhi main-line terminal? This is a daily connection service that arrives only twenty-odd minutes or so before the magnificent yet ageing Viceroy's Toy Train departs on a further six-hour journey to Shimla – the final leg of an arduous yet breathtaking uphill journey that must be endured without the customer comforts of electrical-powered air-conditioning. Even today, as the diesel locomotive slowly and steadily snakes its way through the hills, those passengers not able to afford tickets for the relatively luxurious padded seats of the first-class carriages can be seen huddled together upon hard, rickety wooden bench seats. Numerous others, who were probably late arrivals, quite amazingly seem totally reconciled to their plight, and as a result calmly take up places in the open doorways, many sitting with both legs dangling over the track.

The railway facilities from Kalka to Shimla opened for passenger service on 9 November 1903. Throughout its length of 57 miles there is a continuous succession of reverse curves of 120-feet radius in and out along the valleys and spurs, flanking mountains rising to 6,000 and 7,000 feet above sea level. The steepest gradient of the two-foot narrow-gauge track is three feet in a hundred. The works of construction entailed the boring of 107 tunnels, aggregating 5 miles in length; numerous lofty arched viaducts, aggregating 1¾ miles; and innumerable cuttings and stone walls.[11] Another incredible statistic, which would no doubt please Henry's father, who could look back with satisfaction on all that has been achieved in such a short timescale, is the fact that the Indian Railway is now the biggest employer in the world "moving ten million people in a day, over 6,000 kilometres of track".[12] Inevitably most daily national newspapers, particularly the *Times* of India or the *Hindustani Times*, carry numerous advertisements on behalf of India's various regional Railway Recruitment Boards. Although Shimla, Himachal's capital, is India's largest and most famous hill station, where Rudyard Kipling's colonial classic, *Kim*, took place, it would be totally misleading to give too much weight to the current beauty of the once superlative hillside resort, as it would unquestionably amass justifiable criticism. Modern-day Shimla, with its numerous functional apartment

A gathering of the village elders and probably young reincarnations of indigenous Vaivasis (dwellers of the Himalayan hill forests).

One of the lofty arched viaducts.

blocks that house over 150,000 people, has, as one would expect, taken its toll on the town's extremely regal past. It was often spoken of with "disparaging sobriquets like 'Mount Olympus' and 'Home of the Little Tin Gods'".[13] However, in keeping with the grand colonial Raffles Hotel, now deep within the forever increasing concrete jungle of Singapore, an initial glance at the Victorian Gothic spire of Christ Church, the Viceregal Lodge and the splendid Cecil Hotel, which rather appropriately is situated along the Mall, will immediately generate a certain feel of past majestic Britishness. The Mall, the town's main pedestrian thoroughfare, Shimla's Savile Row, which curves around the south slope of the hillside Ridge, is flanked by a long row of unmistakeably British half-timbered buildings. Further along the Mall, home to many troops of the town's indigenous monkeys, is the quaint Gaiety Theatre, which after current restoration work will look exactly as it did in the heyday of the Raj. The Shimla Amateur Dramatic Club shares the ornate colonial venue with a gentlemen's club where the talk revolves around cricket and share prices.[14] Completed in 1888, the Viceregal Lodge, which crowns Observatory Hill, was the summer seat of British government until as late as the 1940s. Although it is now the home of the Indian Institute of Advanced Study, the splendid lodge depicts Shimla at its most British. "Built in Elizabethan style with a lion and unicorn set above the entrance porch,"[15] the Viceregal Lodge tends to make you feel as you enter the building that you have come through a time warp. Visitors are transported into an era where Britannia not only ruled the waves but very nearly governed the globe.

The rich man in his castle, the poor man at his gate,
God made them, high or lowly, and ordered their estate.

Lord Curzon, Viceroy of India (1899–1905), apparently sang these most appropriate lyrics with great vigour.[16]

A matter of equal significance, and for Henry's parents of greater importance, was that Simla, a British oasis surrounded by twenty-seven hill states of less magnitude, not only and somewhat ironically had a most prodigious estate officially known by many locals and numerous Scottish troops as Stirling Castle, but also benefited from having a Catholic cathedral, the Church of St Michael and St Joseph. Built in the Gothic style, it is cruciform in shape and has a spacious nave and two aisles. Over the high altar is a statue of St Francis of Assisi, showing the stigmatised hands; on the right is a statue of St

The splendid Viceregal Lodge.

Henry loved to ride.

Joseph. The first archbishop was the Most Reverend Anselm E. J. Kenealy, who, as Father Anselm, was well known in England as a lecturer in logic and metaphysics. He was guardian of Crawley Monastery in Sussex, a member of the Oxford Union Society, and provincial of the English province, before being called to Rome as definitor general of his order. Ecclesiastical records, still held at the church, show that on 20 July 1919 his able successor, Father Sylvester Walsh, OSFC, who was also vicar general of the archdiocese dutifully baptised the seventeen-day-old Henry.[17]

Undoubtedly, as years passed by, the very epoch in which the young Henry Stirling matured bore its imprint beside a natural inheritance of unusual parents and the enchanting memories of a wonderful childhood. There was also a terrible simplicity about the order of events that were to follow; privilege and good fortune enriched by marvellous surrounds provided much to admire and emulate and how could anyone possibly fail to understand why? Simla, Henry's birthplace, was essentially an impressive hill of deodars, the beautiful conifers that Kipling and many others before him had described. Yet, as the auspicious Henry gaily strolled the town's busy pathways or rode the hill station's dusty roads, he had so many other trees to admire – oaks, crimson-and-white-flowering rhododendron and its congener the andromeda (bog rosemary), maples, cornus, laurel and roses. And, as soon as he was old enough to hold a rod and safely handle a shotgun, he had around him an abundance of game birds to shoot and fish to catch.

Somewhat inevitably, this idyllic although rather unnaturally isolated childhood meant that a cosseted and indulgent Henry fell hopelessly and deeply in love with both botany and hunting – two intense passions that would steadfastly grow as he did. In striking contrast, however, a true perception of the hardships that life had bestowed on others was indeed very much lacking. And at the time, from all accounts, it seems likely that Henry was not unduly bothered. The silly woes of the world were for argumentative and disagreeable grown-ups. After all, for British children of the Raj, the Indian Empire, still called the *jewel in the colonial crown*, had many splendid hills and wonderful trees to climb, game to shoot and fish to catch, together with laughter and light-hearted fun to seek.

In James Hay Stirling, however, Henry had a father of quiet purpose; and, in spite of possessing shy unassuming characteristics, he was a parent who, although having agreed that Henry should be brought up in the Catholic faith, was nevertheless determined that his son would not escape the customary practice of sending children back to school in England. This tradition inevitably meant that many children would fail to see their parents for several years.

Henry's father also knew that his son, despite having attended a Catholic school for boys established in Simla by the Irish Christian Brothers, needed to understand that in his later years there would not always be servants or ayahs (housemaids or nursemaids) at hand for him to simply call upon when the need arose. However, let there be no misunderstanding over this heart-rending ruling: it did not mean that Henry's parents or indeed others were in any way less loving or concerned. On the contrary, it simply meant that they were determined to provide the best for their offspring by displaying a deep and well-intended sense of parental accountability. Furthermore, added to this resolute parental responsibility, also came a longing that the carefree and untroubled Henry would learn the broad and at times the harsh parodies of life and would also learn them quickly by experience. Knowing and accepting that, in character building, the young must endure pain and pleasure in equal measures, Henry's father presumably stood firm against the wishes of the highly spirited and Henry-doting Blanche. He did what was generally accepted as being proper – he sent his much loved son to England to be taught under strict guidelines and pain of punishment by men of the holy order of a good and extremely well-respected Catholic school. A more than ticklish *downside* would soon enter the pleasurable, almost fantasy world of Henry Hay Dundas Stirling!

Henry and the indomitable Blanche dressed to ride.

CHAPTER TWO

Downside and Peterhouse

ACT I

Bene orasse est bene studuisse – to have prayed well is to have studied well.

Latin proverb

Henry Hay Dundas Stirling entered Downside School in May 1933, having spent several nomadic years at a number of seemingly less impressive preparatory schools that were also back in England. By all accounts it seems that although these establishments were perfectly suitable for Henry's requirements they failed to meet the high standards and expectations of his mother. She considered them to be appallingly administrated, preposterously expensive and therefore all dreadfully overrated. Indeed, the headmaster of one unsuspecting school at the seaside town of Broadstairs was very fortunate not to have been pursued to the high court by a furious Blanche Stirling. As usual the reason for her frustrations surrounded the antics of her eccentric and robust son, who on this particular occasion had either been dared to perform some outrageous act or had been endeavouring to perform do-it-yourself dentistry. Henry, determined not to appear a wimp to his new colleagues or perhaps refusing to follow the school rules on sickness and probably its long-winded procedure, had somehow managed to swallow a hatpin! The commotion and fuss that followed has now entered the realms of family folklore and one wonders whether the poor wretched teacher directly responsible for Henry at the time of the incident actually managed to retain his or her position at the school. Placing eccentricities to one side, however, the out-of-place and dispirited Henry was unquestionably feeling more than just a little uneasy; his new life in England was a strange beginning for a young colonial. More problematic was that his mother's zealous, overprotective demeanour had begun to grow to a most uncomfortable level completely disproportionate to reality. This shortcoming bordered upon uncontrolled hysteria and was to manifest some years later when, to her anger and utter disgust, Henry became one of many thousands who sustained serious injuries during the Second World War. Unlike the earlier incident at Broadstairs, Blanche Stirling, who had insisted upon having the facilities of rented accommodation in nearby Minehead in order to monitor Henry's education, would not fail to take matters further. Moreover, she would subsequently demand to have her views acted upon.

Although clearly spoilt, it appears that many less fortunate classmates had begun to recognise a kindness in young Henry, which prompted more than just an inkling of sympathy for the cosseted and extraordinary Anglo-Indian. In return, Henry gleefully welcomed a chance at Downside. At first it would serve as a well-deserved respite from the arduous strains of forever changing schools. Thereafter stability would provide a sense of belonging and help overcome previous difficulties in the finding of friends and securing companionship. For better or worse, when Henry Hay Dundas signed the class attendance register for the very first time, a redhead thirteen-year-old would from that moment on unwittingly carry the hopes and prayers of a quietly proud and understanding father and the insatiable ambitions of an extremely strong-willed mother.

Downside - Henry is seated in the front row, second from right.

Luckily, as matters panned out, Downside, situated at Stratton-on-the-Fosse, Radstock, Bath, proved to be a most appropriate venue for the hitherto perplexed Henry. It too had originated from a colourful and muddled heritage and had become something of a conundrum. The renowned and accomplished school was actually founded in 1606 at Douai, for English Catholics in exile because of the harsh penal laws. (This very traditional French town, which remains steeped in religious history, holds several re-enactments of Benedictine festivals during the year, although in recent times the town is best known as being the gateway to France.) As religious quarrels abated throughout Britain another equally disrupting phenomenon erupted across the protective Channel – the citizen uprising against the decadent French aristocracy. Sensing the growing and brutal acrimony between the obsolete power of the Monarchists and the nouveau-riche bourgeoisie leaders of aggrieved peasant-stock Republicans, and fearing for the safety of their own well-to-do charges, the Downside masters acted quickly and very appropriately. "At a time of the French Revolution the monks fled to England and in 1814 moved to Downside, where the English Benedictine community of St Gregory settled. It lies on the Mendip Hills in splendid Somerset country, twelve miles from Bath. Handsome buildings and excellent modern facilities make a compact campus of which the monastery and abbey are a part."[1]

Modern-day Downside is probably not too dissimilar to how it was in the period when an unsuspecting Henry Stirling first took refuge from the unquestionable trauma of tiresome itinerancy. Although it is now impossible to compare the school's current facilities with those of yesteryear, it is more than likely that its rigidly enforced discipline code was considerably more punitive than its current code of student conduct. Nevertheless there is no denying that the ecclesiastical tutors at Downside are still extremely intolerant of any hint of unlawful or unacceptable behaviour. One other matter appears not to have changed in spite of our more liberal times: the total irrelevance of status or wealth of any particular student's sponsor, guardian or parent. "Pupils falling behind with work may have some weekend privileges withdrawn; those caught with drugs will be expelled; rustication for bringing alcohol into the school; gating for breaking bounds; bullying leads to expulsion."[2]

According to David Anselan James Dundas Stirling, BA, BL, Henry's only son, who dutifully followed Henry's wishes and

Downside, 1937 – 1st fifteen rugby team. Henry is seated second from left.

Downside. 1937 – 1st eleven hockey team. Henry is seated second from right.

entered Downside during 1961, his father adored his time there, immediately feeling at home. By way of further interest, Henry, who was nominated to serve and give loyal obedience to Roberts House seems to have benefited from several instances of composed tranquillity added to by many moments of spiritual intervention. Needless to say, with such divine guidance and vigorous encouragement from his housemaster, Dom Brendan (who was also the rugby coach and games master), the sports-mad Henry began to excel in all the school's varied activities. This included being able to enjoy the additional paybacks that came with being a trusted school prefect. In a remarkable change of fortune, Henry quickly grew into a gifted sports-loving academic, more than able to hold his own within the presence of older, more senior and, as it happened, much larger competitors. Classified in the sporting cliché as a good all-rounder, talented in disciplines ranging from cricket, rowing, hockey and boxing, the tough, wiry Henry was more than a little special at rugby. His aptitude was especially suited for the fast and furious game of rugby sevens. A passion and skill for the more general game of rugby union, however, not only secured Henry a place in the school's first fifteen, via the colts, but also soon took him to the Somerset town of Minehead to play sevens for its local rugby club.

The Raven, *Downside School Magazine, No. 146, December 1935, Page 22.*

COLTS XV.

The usual team were:
I. F. M. Turnbull, A. D. Keay, N. P. Coke, J. M. Cunningham, A. P. Dodd, W. G. H. Bonham, P. E. Y. Dawson, J. K. Mason, P. O'K. Plumpton, H. H. D. Stirling, W. E. Crowder, P. W. J. Nugent, H. L. Roche-Kelly, T. S. W. Reeve-Tucker and C. Sapieha. D. V. Brennan and S. R. D. Bell also played.

Ironically, some years later the seaside resort chosen by Henry's parents as being a suitable location from where they could monitor their son's every move, and where Henry continued to play sevens for the Barbarians, even while reading at Cambridge, suddenly became a venue of even more significance. At a sheltered spot somewhere upon a sunbaked beach, a smitten Henry would learn a more genteel pastime – the art of falling in love!

With prospects at Downside improving, Henry's next significant achievement was to provide his father with a great deal of satisfaction. And, although his mother acted as though her son was simply complying with her wishes, at the age of only fifteen Henry entered his first Oxbridge examination. His astute tutors had quickly recognised a natural flair for study, and as a result Henry was prematurely entered for several academic subjects. Their supreme confidence in the talented Henry was quickly rewarded. In July 1934 he passed the Oxford and Cambridge Lower Certificate Examination in seven subjects: Latin, French (written & oral), arithmetic, additional mathematics, English, history and geography. Precisely a year thereafter his accomplishments continued unabated. A precursory examination to achieve the Higher Certificate resulted in Henry being presented with a School Diploma from the Oxford and Cambridge Schools Examination Board. He gained four credits in English, Latin, additional mathematics and physics and an equal number of passes in history, French with oral, elementary mathematics, and chemistry. As though these efforts were worthy of greater recognition and acclaim, the Examination Board verified his School Certificate 'A' by awarding additional credits in English, Latin, additional mathematics and physics. As a finale, Henry's efforts brought additional acknowledgement: for his outstanding achievements in both physics and mathematics he was awarded the XII-form prize for outstanding merit. During the end-of-term ceremony, after having vigorously shaken the headmaster's hand, the talented Henry was presented with a magnificent embossed library book inscribed as follows:

COL-S.GREGORII-M-DE-DOWNSIDE.
Henry Stirling: PRAEMIVM-DILIGENTIA-MERITVM in arte mathematica.

Even more satisfying for the accomplished Henry had been the liberty to nominate a book of his choice. As to be expected, Henry's selection was a volume that he would always treasure: *At the Sign of the Split Cane*, by Jock Scott. First published during 1934, the book narrates and illustrates the art of fishing, particularly fly-fishing. It identifies and describes all the known species of flies and provides expert advice on how to obtain success. All in all, Henry could have not made a more appropriate choice.

With these laurels duly won, and with so much praise and achievement surrounding Henry, it would be correct to assume that the Christmas festivities and the Hogmanay celebrations at the end of 1938 were indeed times of true comfort and joy for the family trio. Henry's greatest triumph waited. Having attained all the required grades in his chosen subjects, university beckoned. For his proud parents their prayers had been answered. Not only had Henry excelled at every discipline he had entered, particularly mathematics, but he had matured physically and had become an excellent sportsman. His time at Downside had seen him represent the college at rugby, boxing, athletics and gymnastics. For Henry's devout Catholic mother there was a far deeper consequence. Her constant praying of the rosary and her additional prayers to St Jude, the helper of lost causes, had been received very favourably.

Henry, no longer deemed to be an *enfant perdu* – a lost cause – would very soon be mixing with the educated elite within the walls of a prestigious Cambridge College. In colloquial terms, he had cracked it. He had bravely taken on and won his battle with the keepers of St George, the aristocratic English, one of whom was a boxing chum and one-time golden boy of the Conservative Party and the bar, Peter Anthony Grayson Rawlinson, Lord Rawlinson of Ewell, born 26 June 1919, died 28 June 2006. As a consequence he had shown that colonial schoolboys were not a group of second-rate radicals who had ventured to intrude. Neither were they a bunch of unimaginative *Delhi-wallahs* more suited to the rough and tumble of His Majesty's Armed Forces, but a faction of well-versed and loyal patriots who were also very capable of holding their own in academia.

Even at the peak of his success, however, there was another, more pessimistic, side to Henry – a remarkable understanding of how rapidly the world was changing. He had begun to recognise the start of an age where the first shoots of independence had begun to entwine with the ailing system of the Raj. In spite of his prospects improving, seemingly at every turn, changes had already begun to cause problems. Henry had one dream above all others: to return after his studies to the magnificent grandeur of the Kashmir. What would ultimately follow was obvious; whilst in England he would have found a supportive, beautiful and somewhat obedient wife. The next proceedings of his carefully orchestrated life would entail a trip back to India and as many children as the good Lord decreed. Furthermore he would work for the Indian Forestry Service, and whilst at work he would bask within and enjoy his first and foremost love, the superlative splendour of the lower Himalayan countryside awash with woodland, lakes and, of course, fish.

The storm clouds above India were darkening rapidly, and even before the outbreak of war many Indian authorities were beginning to defy and whittle away at British Imperialism. For a while at least both Hindus and Muslims appeared united and had begun to uniformly shout cries of *"Jai Hind,"* meaning may India flourish.

The gusto for change had led to a matter of direct significance. To quote from a letter written by Henry, who appears from the tone to be both bemused and frustrated, the Indian Forestry Service was to be Indianised, thus making his prospective and longed-for degree in forestry somewhat unnecessary. In a pique of temper, sensing the folly of cloaked anti-British slogans proclaiming *'Hindu Muslim ek tio'* – Hindus and Muslims are one – Henry looked towards the future and quite naturally focused upon the previous achievements of his highly successful father. Subsequently, and extremely sensibly, he accepted what was ultimately inevitable and turned to a tried and tested subject in which he was equally most qualified. He decided to study for a degree in the science of engineering.

ACT II

'Its distance from the rest of the university has been more than just geographical. Cambridge has always held itself aloof from the rest of the country. In the eighties it was the penultimate college to accept women, and the site of the bloodiest battle to prevent their admission.'

Michael Gove

The next stage of Henry's preparation for a moral and prosperous life, in strict accordance with the schedule devised by his parents, was to be his matriculation into Peterhouse College during the autumn of 1938, on scholarship in mechanical science.[2] To recap upon his academic record thus far, he had performed exceedingly well in his finals at Downside having attained Higher Certificates, grade A, in three subjects (English, chemistry and physics) with earlier passes in three subsidiary disciplines (mathematics, physics and chemistry). A sound achievement was added in the March of that year when he attained a pass in the qualifying examination, mechanical sciences tripos.[3]

Taking time out as a gentleman gamekeeper.

Peterhouse was founded in 1284 by His Eminence Hugo de Balsham, Bishop of Ely, thereby placing the ornate establishment in the unique position of being the oldest university college in Cambridge. At the centre of the old part of the college is the Chapel, a monument that acclaims the proud traditions of college life: prayer, enquiry, creativity and community.[4] On reflection, Peterhouse was the perfect setting for Henry's final academic learning; the college had all the correct essentials that could build upon his strong theological beliefs, his astute intellectual prowess and his brilliantly inquisitive mind.

Apparently, during Henry's time at Peterhouse the rather quaint establishment had not overtly developed into the rather mysterious and political institution of more recent times. This point was made quite candidly by Michael Gove, a political journalist, who in 1995 wrote *The Future of the Right*, a biography of the one-time 'darling of the Conservative Party', the captivating Michael Portillo. During an explicit description of the college, his tone clearly suggests that the college is somewhat notorious for its political persuasions: "One of the smallest, and the most secretive colleges in Cambridge, Peterhouse produced a number of figures whose public influence shaped the Toryism of the Thatcher years."[5]

Any recall upon Henry's time in India, as a child of the Raj, makes an explanation as to why he eventually chose the science of engineering as an alternative to botanical forestry rather straightforward. Notwithstanding his passion for plants and wildlife, during his formative years he had also witnessed a huge transformation of his beloved India. Moreover, and no doubt with a touch of uneasiness, he had also recognised that, apart from the unpleasant changes to the political landscape, other far-reaching and on the whole beneficial changes had originated from the construction of the railways that his talented father had gone some way to introduce. Furthermore and not least, another aspect played its part. The decision to carry forward the family profession or trade, in particular the skills of his father, was a hugely popular and most acceptable one.

Apart from his father's influence, however, other telling factors require debate. Whereas Henry followed the arts and other more prodigious subjects with a questioning mind, a keen eye and at times a sharp tongue, his interest in serious politics and intricate law was especially limited. He was a staunch imperialistic conservative in the Churchillian mode, and the British political scene before, during and after the war would have undeniably angered him.

He would have agreed with Churchill, who, during a speech at the Mansion House Dinner in November 1942, growled angrily, "We mean to hold our own. I have not become the King's first minister to preside over the liquidation of the British Empire."[6] Although another flagrant use of hindsight, the break-up and eventual partition of glorious India, the jewel in the British crown, and the quarrels over his beloved Kashmir unquestionably stunned and hurt Henry. In spite of once admiring the mulish stubbornness of Gandhi, he, like Churchill and numerous others, feared the onset of religious tension, especially if further autonomy was granted to the vast subcontinent. Subsequently Henry had been against India's quest for Dominion status within the British Commonwealth and Empire, in keeping with Canada, Australia and the troubled Union of South Africa where Gandhi had once practised law. Born into a particularly grand Anglo-Indian society, Henry would have no doubt been equally horrified at Gandhi's outrageous dress code. The appearance of a world leader adorned only by an extremely modest loincloth would have been simply unbecoming. And Gandhi's disturbing habit of frequently attending more formal, indeed royal, occasions while so very scantily dressed would have amounted to nothing less than gross disrespect – especially as Gandhi was well aware of British etiquette, having graduated from the University of London.

Furthermore, should fate have played its part and Henry had entered Parliament as another 'blue' offspring from Cambridge, what would have been his attitude to those interfering party whips, so ably described by Jeremy Paxman as bullying "keepers of parliament's dark secrets and custodians of the baubles of public life"?[7] More especially, their nauseating practice, known in various areas of discipline as the 'carrot and stick' ideology, used in parliamentary terms as a method of maintaining clonish discipline and securing sufficient votes on spurious legislation. Well aware that politics is very often a contest of wills, Henry would have no doubt learnt how to nullify any undue pressure, however unpleasant, and would have easily ignored the possibilities of earning a parliamentary favour, such as a bogus fact-finding mission abroad, somewhere lavish (of course) and blessed with copious hours of sunshine. As a result, a resolute and honourable Henry would have acted in a manner that in truth could only be described as downright defiance. And at some stage during his short political career he would have caused mayhem, either by open rebellion or by making a statement of disagreement to a packed and stunned House of

Commons. Even though Henry would have probably spoken eloquently, combining fortitude with great charm, humour and a sprinkling of Latin verse that would fly over the heads of the bemused party opposite, ruthless retribution would have followed and his political life would have soon ended.

Almost certainly and unlike Henry's contemporary, the essentially right-wing maverick, the Conservative Member for Bromley and Chislehurst, the Right Honourable Eric Forth, MP, who died suddenly of cancer during May 2006, Henry would not have given one inch to any political compromise. Both Henry and the Glaswegian Eric Forth originated from the same knowledgeable and satirical mould. The extravagantly attired nonconformist vigorously questioned mainstream opinion and cleverly ridiculed modern, relatively slick American clichés, but Henry's acute single-mindedness would have caused much the greater annoyance. This would have been true, not only in relation to members opposite, but also in respect of his own party colleagues, most of whom would have feared for their parliamentary careers and personal financial security. Another matter upon which there could be certainty: it would have been quite unimaginable for Henry to have been selected to hold a prominent position within the inner sanctum of the Privy Council.

Taking up the possibility of Henry qualifying for the Bar, his overriding approach to his duties would certainly be reminiscent of those few telling words once spoken by Churchill when the great man described Mother Russia as a kind of puzzling riddle wrapped in an enigma! The greedy or foolish stupidity of some woolly-minded victims of criminal deception would have angered him. The act of defending overtly guilty perpetrators of gratuitous violence would have been totally dishonourable in his virtuous view and the very thought of others within his own chambers actually agreeing to do so would have caused him acute nausea. On the other hand, briefs detailing a variety of the most ingenious scams that underpinned well-executed company frauds would have definitely offered a fitting challenge to his sharp, rational mind and his undeniable wisdom, but their tiresome longevity would have eventually bored him. Moreover, Henry's unwavering ethics aided by a calm inner confidence would have surely clashed with the insatiable and at times unprincipled antics of the overinflated barrister's clerk.

Placing all such vivid conjecture to one side, however, Henry, aware that a wonderful life immersed in Indian Kashmir was now nothing more than a pipe dream, somewhat reluctantly took up residency at Peterhouse on 9 October 1938. Sadly little else is known of this short period of learning, although the College Register clearly shows that he took to his studies exceedingly well before requesting permission to suspend his studies in order that he too could follow his government's bold decision to restore hope and justice to a threatened and vulnerable Europe. After having obtained the necessary concessions, Henry, by now something of an individualist and always eccentrically apart from others, would no doubt have hurried towards the hallowed grounds of the college, sworn an oath of allegiance to God and country before making a very personal declaration of war against Hitler's Germany.

Unquestionably, it was Henry's sudden and unnecessary decision to volunteer for active service and eventually take up a commission in the Royal Artillery that temporarily rang the death knell for his mother's persuasive endeavours. Ever since conflict had become increasingly more likely she had worked tirelessly to implant in her son's mind that any future war would not be an Irish Free State issue and that Henry should stop acting as if he were a grievously harmed Englishmen, offended by German Imperialism. Subsequently, after Henry had stubbornly refused to agree and had volunteered for the British Army, there was to be little joy in future family gatherings. Selfish as his decision may have seemed to his adoring parents, Henry's time at Downside and his short stay at Peterhouse had helped him to acquire a new strength of character and an air of independence. He was no longer in a position where he could be easily protected by his overbearing mother or gently coerced by his father's influence. At last he felt free. Again with a distinct sense of paradoxical irony, the Catholic Henry Hay Dundas Stirling, a descendant of Sir William Stirling 1st of Keir, would on attestation first swear the oath of faithful and true allegiance to an English Protestant monarch, His Majesty King George VI, before preparing his woad for combat.

Rowing was another of Henry's passions – he is seated fifth up from the cox.

CHAPTER THREE

War, Wife and Wounded

ACT I

'This is not a question of fighting for Danzig or fighting for Poland. We are fighting to save the whole world from the pestilence of Nazi tyranny and in defence of all that is most sacred to man. This is no war of domination or imperial aggrandizement or material gain; no war to shut any country out of its sunlight and means of progress. It is a war, viewed in its inherent quality, to establish, on impregnable rocks, the rights of the individual, and it is a war to establish and revive the stature of man.'
Winston Churchill to the House of Commons,
3 September 1939

Those who believe that all old soldiers like to reminisce about their own particular, and very often their own unique, experience of war may be surprised to know that in the company of Henry Hay Dundas Stirling the subject was strictly taboo. It was as if the rather macho topic was still cloaked under wraps of clandestine British military intelligence or still fell within the remit of sub judice within some military courtroom drama. Another issue that was so very obvious was that tight-lipped Henry had studied his service manual in some depth and remembered the interpersonal skills required of the officer ranks. He fully understood the relevance of those curt, punchy wartime clichés such as "Careless talk costs lives" and "No names, no pack drill".

Never a soldier at heart, Henry hated war and its utter destructiveness. He knew that in times of war both conflict and strife multiply like a cancerous growth vigorously gnawing away at futile boundaries, thus affecting blameless peace-loving countries as well as belligerent nations. Furthermore, he realised that many innocents would unnecessarily lose their lives, and others their homes, pets and livestock. As a botanist in the making he dreaded the thought of countless meadows and wildlife being savagely raped by a constant rain of bombs and shells. The knowledge of how woodland, lakes and rivers had been scarred and polluted by the enormity of war's debris was for Henry simply too much to bear. And, as a keen environmentalist, the loss of much treasured countryside was just too horrid to contemplate. Opinions must inevitably vary as to the greatest hardships that result from war, yet it is extremely easy to understand why the Second World War or any conflict thereafter was never considered as being a suitable after-dinner theme.

Although the National Service Act, passed by Parliament on the first day of the war, had decreed universal and compulsory conscription, Henry's sudden decision to volunteer for active service was not taken lightly. Rather than a mood of flippant impulsiveness there was a genuine and caring thought of doing what was right. Articles discussing the dilemma over university students and the call-up, which had began to worry the academic boffins within the Ministry of Labour and the War Office, did not therefore apply. Henry, who immediately put himself forward to appear before the Cambridge University Joint Recruiting Board could always recognise dangerous folly in the making. He had sensed that once again Europe was in peril, and that Britannia and its global Empire were vulnerable. Aware that the Spanish Civil War had unmistakably drawn Fascist Italy even closer to the scourge of National Socialist Germany, he could foresee the development of an unholy and destructive trinity. More so, Henry was astute enough to look beyond the veneer of prosperity that tended to conceal the true dictatorial aims of Europe's political ultra-right. Not one for missing out on ventures new, Henry was absolutely determined to have a role in the downfall of the flamboyant and vulgar Italian, Benito Amilcare Mussolini, who absurdly answered to the title *Duce*, or leader, and of that appalling little Austrian upstart called Adolf Hitler. The chivalrous Henry had yet another sense of urgency over the need to restore democracy to the foolish German people by casting out the evil induced by Hitler and his Nazis. An iniquitous spell had mesmerised an entire nation and had made millions believe that they were all descendants of Aryan warrior gods, and that Hitler was not only their chosen Führer, but also a god in his own right. To Henry, the very thought that perfectly sane normal German folk could consume such trite nonsense was not only madness but was utterly preposterous; to Henry Stirling, only the likes of Churchill and Imperial Britain, which still governed the wonderfully majestic Indian subcontinent, and had done so since 1 January 1877 when Queen Victoria was officially crowned Empress, could possibly have grounds for such a claim.

Regardless of Henry's colourful caricature of European politics, it was his unwillingness to speak glibly about the Second World War that has made it impossible to provide a detailed narrative of his own particular exploits. Another issue that undeniably complicates matters, especially after Henry had been wounded, was his rather odd decision not to amend particulars of his next of kin after he had married. Whether or not this factor was just an oversight remains uncertain, yet, as matters stood, despite Henry's relatively new marital status, his father James remained the official nominee. And, as additional problems unfolded due to Henry's whereabouts, more confusion arose over his contact address continuing to be the family home in Jodhpur, Rajputana.

To some degree, however, enquiries with the Ministry of Defence have managed to unravel a period in Henry's life that has hitherto been cloaked in mystery. Inevitably, though, the records are rather scant. "Unfortunately there is no mention of his time in Cairo. As previously mentioned the Army Service Record is often brief and simply traces the individual's service career. Only very rarely does the file mention places visited or action seen."[1]

On 26 September 1939, just twenty-three days after Britain declared war on Germany, the Cambridge University Joint Recruiting Board recommended that the volunteer Henry be trained as an officer in the Royal Artillery. His candidacy had been greatly encouraged by his former headmaster at Downside, an eminent JP for Somerset, who provided testimonies as to his suitability to serve as an officer and of his high moral character.

Subsequently, Henry followed a standardised procedure: as an aspiring officer he should spend some time in the ranks, thereby earning the recommendation of the unit's commanding officer. Thereafter, as a successful candidate, he would be accepted as an officer cadet and spend a relatively short period in intensive training. The actual length of training very much depended on the arm of the service; it was, however, about four to six months.

Consequently, on 18 July 1940, after preliminary assessment the jubilant Henry was recommended as being a suitable applicant for officer cadet training.

As an aside, it appears that this vetting procedure was to some extent wayward. Without national guidelines, the chances of prospective candidates achieving success became somewhat of a lottery. All applicants, despite having valued and suitable qualifications, were still very much dependent on the whims and opinions of their respective interviewers. This unsatisfactory situation, along with the inevitable 'who you knew' factor, had understandably led to some excellent men being rejected while the more astute and socially aware among them simply refrained from volunteering. Meanwhile, it is also true to mention that any in-depth study into officer recruitment of the period also tends to suggest a lingering of the highly influential First World War adage: 'It's class and background that counts.'

RECORD OF TRAINING UNDERGONE BY
No. 931639 Gnr. STIRLING H. H. D.
Date of joining: 18.7.40

(a) Passed out in Foot and Rifle Drill including Ceremonial and Tactical Guard Duties.
(b) Fired Recruits Course Musketry .303 on open range. Instructed in Lewis Gun (not fired).
(c) 10 weeks Gun Drill and Laying. Knows work of all gun numbers and is a fair layer.
(d) Elementary training in Director and Specialist Work.
(e) Map reading to standard of 1st Class Gunner.
(f) Completed Gas Training.
(g) Elementary knowledge of interior economy of a Battery administrative duties and responsibilities of a section Commander.

B. G. P. Sunderland
Lieut. Col. R.A.
Commanding 16 Field Training Regiment. R.A.[2]

Having successfully completed a period of intense training with the 16 Field Training Regiment, Royal Artillery, Henry's overall assessment was initially classified as being 'very suitable', and his medical category was deemed 'A1'.

Subsequently, on 21 March 1941, only a few weeks before his wedding, and as if every member of staff at the training school was fully aware of his intentions to personify the event as a chivalrous officer and gentleman, Henry, whose final assessment was 'very fair', was granted a commission to 2nd Lieutenant, Royal Artillery. Thereafter he was assigned for immediate active serve in the Middle East.[3]

On 20 September 1941, within six short months, Henry was disembarking in Egypt. Whatever else may have occurred upon his arrival is uncertain, but records show that for the unfortunate Henry there would be little time for fun or sightseeing. He was immediately posted to serve with 68th Medium Regiment, Royal Artillery. An ironic and interesting point, which becomes more relevant particularly towards the end of his military career when confusion as to his whereabouts arose, was that this artillery unit was seconded to support elements of the 4th Indian Division. Another matter arising from military records is that Henry's ability to ride was also duly noted, thus making parts of his misspent youth, particularly the playing of polo, extremely worthwhile. Having been granted a King's commission he had specifically expressed a preference for active service with an Indian army unit.[4]

At this point, and without wishing to stray too far from Henry's future heroics, it may be helpful to provide a short précis detailing the wide format of the British Army and highlighting the particular role of the Royal Artillery.

During the Second World War, the British Army was comprised of the old Regular, Territorial and Airborne divisions, as well as County divisions that were speedily formed for key defence duties along Britain's highly vulnerable coast. In addition there were the loyal armies of the Commonwealth, including, of most relevance to Henry's position, the steadfast divisions of the Indian Army.

Commissioned or enlisted artillerymen, all known as gunners, would join specifically numbered Royal Artillery units and each regiment would perform any one of several important yet somewhat divergent roles. These would range from anti-tank or anti-aircraft responsibilities to medium and large field-artillery duties. Another point of possible significance is that artillery officers were very often called upon to provide additional and vital communicative skills on a battlefield. This was an essential factor, bearing in mind the importance of having clear unambiguous communiqués and the range and effectiveness of modern ordnance. Finally, although unlikely

An officer and a gentleman.

Competing in a relay changeover during a Royal Artillery sports day.

to have had any true sway upon Henry's subsequent posting, some regiments – previously horse cavalry – had been integrated into the Royal Regiment although strictly speaking they were not artillery.

ACT II

'Betty, your trip to Minehead will be the very first holiday that we have not taken together. I have no doubt that once there you will immediately meet the man of your dreams and return eager to marry.'

Lady Trevaskis

Most friends are usually reluctant to divulge too much detail of their formative years. Lady Sheila Trevaskis, wife of Sir Kennedy Trevaskis (a former Ambassador to Aden) and a close friend of Betty Stirling since their schooldays, is one exception to that rule. With a glint in her eye that defies her true age – a matter that quite rightly will no longer be discussed – she remembers Betty and Henry's seaside assignation extremely well. She recalled how Betty, who had ventured to picturesque Minehead, a pleasant West Country resort on the Somerset coast during the summer of 1940, had purely by chance met a most handsome and quite dashing officer in the Royal Artillery. Lady T, as she is still affectionately called, also remembers that, in spite of their short time together, both Betty and Henry were smitten. No one and no circumstance would be able to break their impulsive devotion for each other. The die had been cast; they would be wed as soon as practicable and live happily ever after. Furthermore, the couple would ignore the opinions of all others whether for or against their union.

All this wonderful joy and romantic bliss was soon immeasurably clouded by heated family quarrels. As matters stood, Henry according to his doting mother was far too young to even ponder marriage. Though times have changed, nothing was more natural back in the late thirties or forties than for parents to disagree over their offspring's choice of friends and companions. In relation to a prospective spouse the issue called for greater scrutiny, including a questionnaire upon standing, wealth and, inevitably, religion. Betty Hawley, an Anglican, was a former pupil of St Mary's Abbey, Mill Hill, a matter not taken kindly to by Henry's devout Catholic mother. Sparks flew, but – so typical of the couple – they simply lowered their heads, hugged each

Minehead Barbarians, 1939–1940.
Henry is standing in centre position. His close friend, Dr Michael
Raymond, is to the left (hands behind back, collar up and rolled sleeves).

other for comfort and reassurance, and watched the glowing embers of disagreeableness fly above them. They had made a solemn pact that they would remain steadfast and true.

Unluckily for Henry, in 1941, the year he had chosen to marry and, as the old saying goes, settle down, another significant appointment was being arranged. Much to Henry's annoyance that buffoon Hitler was having incredible success. Even more upsetting was that he had decided to dispatch Lieutenant General Rommel to Tripoli, to bolster the collapsing Italians. With an advanced attachment of what would become the Afrika Korps the intrepid Rommel had been ordered to conduct an aggressive defence of the region. History now recalls that Rommel's campaign was anything but defensive. By 10 April, General Sir Richard O'Connor, the architect of earlier British victories, had been captured and Tobruk was under siege. In just two months, the chance of the British clearing the Axis forces from North Africa had been thrown away. So great was Rommel's success that within eighteen months he had become a legend. Known to the Allies as the Desert Fox, on 22 June of the following year he was appointed Field Marshal.[5]

To recap on events, it was to the hostile environment of North Africa that the love-stricken Henry was posted. It is impossible to tell, but his initial reaction would have probably been fused with a melange of excitement and pride, tinged with much disappointment. Nevertheless, without any further to-do, within forty-eight hours Henry had requested compassionate leave from his unit in order that he could marry, and had arranged a church licence. To his great delight the application was granted and Henry and his pal William Lewis made haste for St Philip's Catholic Church, Finchley, North London. What actually occurred to perhaps allay the worst fears of both Henry's shocked parents and the stunned Hawleys cannot be established with any certainty. However, let there be no misunderstanding: Henry's powerful mastery and persuasive charm could if need be sway the most prickly of characters, let alone the loving and caring Hawleys, who were naturally worried over the whole whirlwind affair. Furthermore, as non-Catholics they had other matters to come to terms with.

Far more worrying, though, was that the war in Europe was going particularly badly thus making their concerns quite reasonable. The odds for any future marriage withstanding the immense external pressures of world conflict were very slim indeed. In respect of Henry's parents, one accusation that could be levelled was folie de grandeur. However, in imagining themselves of higher status they could not have been further from the truth. In keeping with the vast majority of their generation they would have remembered the dreadful carnage of the Great War, where thousands of young men perished over a futile attempt to secure less than fifteen feet of barren wasteland. Without doubt both they and the Hawleys would have prayed in earnest that such a tragedy would never again enter their lives. Consequently, for Henry to be so bullish over going to war after having recently committed himself to the sanctity of marriage, appeared more than just bizarre. It was, in the opinion of their cautious and anxious minds, totally incomprehensible.

Above all these complex issues of personalities, on 3 May 1941, 2nd Lieutenant Henry Hay Dundas Stirling, RA, only son of Mr and Mrs J. H. Stirling of Jodhpur, India, and Miss Betty Hawley, second daughter of Mr and Mrs Harold Hawley of 20 Harvey Close, Finchley, were joined together in holy matrimony. Betty, as unrepentant as the chivalrous Henry, and looking every inch a thoroughly independent and modern woman, chose a bridal gown in pastel blue with hat to match. The gown was suitably adorned with a spray of orchids. The best man was Henry's chum from the same regiment, 2nd Lieutenant William Lewis, RA.[6] They proudly wore uniforms of rank. A number of other close friends attended the ceremony and were invited back to a cocktail party at Betty's parents' home. Despite great diversity, the fairy-tale sequel to love at first sight, which would have been far more appropriate on a filmset in Hollywood rather than Blitz-scarred London, had finally ended.

With celebrations over, a proud and blissfully happy Henry, who was probably acting out and reciting gaudeamus igitur (let us rejoice), bade his farewells. Immediately thereafter, he and his young bride returned to their first love nest, the seaside town of Minehead. Little purpose would be served by continuing to describe their honeymoon romance but one can well imagine the sheer joyousness of strolling hand in hand along the esplanade that commands a wide sweep of the bay. Suffice to say that, for the two lovers, their short honeymoon and the following few months passed by far too quickly. 'Braveheart' Stirling had received notice to discharge himself from one important engagement to another. The forthcoming assignation, however, would be many hundreds of miles from the sandy shores of North Somerset; he was destined for the sand dunes of North Africa, where he and his loyal Indian colleagues had wrongs to right, scores to settle and a war to win!

ACT III

I wondered where he'd been; then heard him shout,
'They snipe like hell! O Dickie, don't go out . . . . '
I fell asleep . . . . Next morning he was dead;
And some Slight Wound lay smiling on the bed.
from *Died of Wounds* by Siegfried Sassoon

One of Henry's few misfortunes was that his wartime deeds were seldom discussed in any real depth or sensible proportion. With the carefree Henry always very willing to talk about more

The wedding party, May 1941.

The bride and groom, May 1941.

light-hearted issues, where fun and laughter was the order of the day, the true seriousness of his first brief rendezvous with possible death was hardly ever recognised. On the few occasions that his time in North Africa did come to the fore, ensuing comments usually prompted exaggerated tales of bad judgement or reluctant foolhardy practice on the part of Henry's slapdash and most wretched driver. Although only informed speculation, the word on Henry's ill-fated desert sojourn was that it probably occurred during the November of 1941 in Libya when the isolated Tobruk garrison took the offensive in an attempt to link up with the advancing British units from the south. Should the anonymous source be correct, it seems extremely likely that Henry took part in Operation Cruader, the second British Libyan Campaign, which began on 18 November 1941. There were two operations: a main attack toward Tobruk, its mission to smash the Axis forces; and a secondary offensive to contain Axis forces in and around the Omar–Halfaya Pass area. On 23/24 November, around the period Henry was wounded, fortified positions in the Omar area were attacked and reduced by units of the 4th Indian Infantry Division despite fierce opposition.[7]

Although Axis forces continued to enjoy some limited success, especially when Crusader faltered and near panic resulted, British forces, led by the hapless Field Marshal Auchinleck (who was replaced by General Alexander and Lieutenant General Montgomery), finally managed to press home the daring offensive. Subsequently, by 10 December, Henry's sterling efforts, whatever they may have been, were graciously rewarded; the siege of Tobruk had been lifted and Rommel had been pushed back to his El Agheila stronghold.

Although less authenticity can be placed on just how Henry was injured, from all accounts it does seems likely that this was due to the carelessness of his blameworthy driver, who by chance had stumbled upon an incorrect route at a most inappropriate time – a driving performance that apparently annoyed Henry intensely. Best forgotten are the amusing rumours of how the belligerent Henry was even more upset by the stark reality of having been shot in the leg by either a dreadfully lucky Italian infantryman, who was obviously taking aim at someone else, or by strafing fire from an Italian aircraft piloted by an equally lucky Italian who was clearly lost and had fired in error. Unquestionably, if the proud Henry had been given a choice, his demise would have most certainly occurred under different circumstances, and then only after many years of gallantry as opposed to a biblical period of forty-odd days!

Having little time for Italian politics then or during his latter years, Henry would have much preferred to have suffered at the hands of a brave yet reckless German panzer grenadier wearing his silver Close Combat Badge or by a highly decorated pilot from the splendid ranks of Hermann Goering's mighty Luftwaffe.

Just how the luckless Henry sustained an injury whilst fighting Rommel's Afrika Korps remains an affair that is still shrouded by myth and mystery. Although this dilemma is equally true in relation to the gravity and extent of the shooting injury, a British Indian passport, issued 16 September 1944, helps provide some degree of corroborative evidence. In addition to granting and thereby extending Henry's right to residency within the Kashmir, the particularly ornate document also reveals that Henry, upon application to the issuing authorities, had declared that there was a highly visible, and as such distinguishing, scar upon his left knee.

Amid conjecture and rumour, there remains another event that can be accepted with more or less certainty: Henry's eventual transfer to a Cairo hospital and leave centre during the war. Having sustained a serious gunshot wound to the knee, Henry would have unquestionably required urgent medical attention, and as a result would probably have been treated by an orthopaedic surgeon at one of the emergency field dressing stations. Thereafter and once able to travel his next step would have been reception at one of the many casualty clearing stations where upon arrival he would have been officially recorded as S.O.S. or T.O.S. (struck or taken of strength). With documentation over, and when transport could have been arranged, Henry would have been taken by ambulance to a Cairo hospital or one of the hastily erected general field hospitals. With Henry's personal sway, aided and abetted by his family connections, it can be presumed that Henry was subsequently given the very best attention by the medical staff of Kasr el Ainy, the city's oldest and most enchanting hospital. This centre of medical excellence, now called the Kasr el Ainy Medical School – Cairo University Hospital, was originally constructed in 1936. Its most striking feature, and one that still instils a sense of the power and glamour of the pre-war colonial period, is the splendid and lofty Italian-designed collegiate church that overlooks the expansive hospital grounds, where crowds seem to huddle around absurdly as if totally mesmerised by the ambience.

Throughout his period of hospitalisation it is unlikely that the dispirited Henry had any idea of the schemes that his worried and intensely furious mother was contriving. With many Allied troops buried at Cairo's nearby Heliopolis War Cemetery, having tended to the immediate business of survival, Henry was probably far too busy contemplating how lucky he had been not to have died from his wounds. And, like most other injured troops, he must have wondered how quickly he could get back to his regiment and rejoin his new family of trusted brothers. Although Henry was probably having immense fun teasing the nursing staff with humorous stories of past British endeavours by adding that old wartime yarn about 'heroes run in my family', it remains highly unlikely that Henry could ever bestow forgiveness upon his poor nameless driver. Probably still smarting over his earlier misfortune, it was to irk Henry that he was to play no further part in the campaign to free North Africa of the tiresome Rommel. He had made a vow that he would wear his Celtic woad with pride, and yet thus far matters on the battlefield had not gone as he would have hoped, nor as he had expected.

As it happened, Henry's sense of comedy over having war heroes within the family was perfectly true. The unassuming John Hugh Saffery, an amateur pilot in his thirties and Henry's very likeable first cousin on his father's side, fitted the description particularly well. Through his passion for and skill of flying John was accepted as a pilot in the war when otherwise his age and eyesight would have let him down. He served in the RAF Reconnaissance Unit, usually flying Spitfires, and was subsequently awarded the DSO and Croix de Guerre (Belge). Once, just after setting out on one of his many heroic sorties over occupied Europe, he was forced to bale out in the Channel and spent sixteen anxious hours before rescue came.

Added to Henry's unsettling disappointment was a genuine concern for his friend and best man at his wedding, 2nd Lieutenant William Lewis. It appears that Henry knew that the unlucky William had also suffered at the hands of the audacious Rommel. Although uninjured, at some stage of the intense campaign he had been taken prisoner.

More uncertainty was to follow. As soon as Henry was able to stand without the aid of crutches, and he was officially deemed ambulatory, he was given some rather startling news. Somehow, and by some unknown means, his well-connected mother had pulled strings and pulled them tightly. The impetuous Blanche Stirling had been extremely busy networking amongst the good and the great, and as a result she was determined that on this occasion her foolhardy Irish charge would listen and obey her wishes. Accordingly, and in spite of being officially invalided out of the Middle East, Henry, a nephew of Vice Admiral Anselan John Buchanan Stirling, CB (1916), Officer of the Legion of Honour and Order of St Anne of Russia with swords – Battle at Jutland – was possibly no longer a wounded British officer.[10] At a stroke, he had most likely become an injury-stricken young man from County Mayo, on the west coast of Ireland who had foolishly entered a war, not of his making, and had paid a dreadful price. One other glaring oversight that altogether ridiculed the spurious suggestion was the military exploits of another uncle of Henry's, his namesake, Lieutenant Colonel Henry Francis Dundas Stirling, MC (military cross), 59th Scinde Rifles, educated at King William's College, IOM, and Sandhurst, and killed in action during 1917. (The 59th Scinde Rifles, founded in the Punjab in 1903, was a volunteer Frontier Force regiment, allied to the Argyll and Sutherland Highlanders.) Indeed, it was the memory of his much-loved brother that was to prompt Henry's father to so christen Henry.[10]

Set against all this absurdity as to Henry's true nationality, and mirroring the uncertainty over his unfortunate experience with enemy gunfire, this truly bizarre conundrum remains clouded by a shroud of myth and mystery, although one aspect is certainly true. Once Henry was invalided from the Middle East he did not, as one would expect, return to England to reassure and to comfort his beautiful Betty; he was unceremoniously dispatched to the relative safety of India. His highly respected and vastly qualified mother had, in colloquial terms, worked the oracle and had performed wonders. Having most likely guaranteed the British military authorities that dealt with reassignments or repatriation that her foolish son would travel to India at his own expense, and after having made it perfectly clear that she would personally oversee his medical and financial welfare, the bemused Henry set sail.

On his arrival in British Kashmir, sandwiched between the Punjab and Nepal, and well away from the interference of the annoying military, Henry was tasked with a hectic programme of recuperation. First and foremost he would maintain all previous effort put into study. Meanwhile, in any spare time, for recreation and reward he would immediately reject the folly of continuing any form of romance by energetically shooting game and instead pursue a passion much more to his mother's liking – fishing. Furthermore, any future displays of irrational behaviour would be forbidden, including any form of jingoistic gallantry. Other conditions were also strictly imposed: he was to vigorously engage in this unexpected opportunity until he was fully recovered from the trials of combat and a kidney infection that had become increasingly tiresome. Then, and in spite of any recovery that he may make, he would wait patiently until the war ended. Then and only then would he be allowed back to the woes he had made for himself in London.

Under considerable strain, and feeling most wretched, Henry was systematically subjected to one condition after another. Yet much worse was to follow. As a finale, the distraught Henry, who was obviously unwell, was eventually diagnosed with hydronephrosis of the left kidney, a medical condition that was to plague him for several years and a problem that would eventually put an end to his military career.

Sweeping aside all possible ifs and buts on this delicate issue there is one certainty. With Henry's doting mother doubling as his private medical consultant, any army medical board tasked to assess and decide upon her beloved son's fitness for further combat would have encountered considerable difficulty and intense scrutiny. Unquestionably Henry's mother would have been on extremely intimate terms with her military colleagues and would have been more than capable of presenting a worst-case scenario. Evidence is so obviously apparent within Henry's service file. Early medical records reveal that, during March 1943, the injured Henry had attended two medical boards. Curiously enough, the final assessment upon his fitness to return to duties and hostilities was in complete contradiction to the first. In spite of this quite appalling muddle, the very existence of these findings helps to unravel one issue of uncertainty, in as much as the bemused Henry, although now in India, was still a serving British officer. Just how and why he was actually allowed to remain in India in order to convalesce is unknown, but it was probably due to the 'who you know' influence of his extremely well-connected mother!

Although perfectly understandable, it would still be misleading and far too simplistic to brand Henry's father as weak-willed and browbeaten, by having possibly allowed his wife to cleverly hoodwink the British military and to be so domineering in respect of Henry's future. This curt and insensitive description fails to sit comfortably with that of a caring and sick father, who in the bloodstained muddy soil of Flanders, during the tragic madness of the Great War, had suffered the loss of a brave and dear brother. The words are equally unsuitable when full consideration is given to the difficult plight of his headstrong and obstinate son.

Many parents would passionately argue that Henry's loving father simply had no other option. Initially, he had been confronted with the worrying news that his only child had been shot during active service in the desert. Thereafter events were equally distressing. Owing to particularly unpleasant renal complications it had been deemed necessary for his wounded offspring to be confined to a hospital bed for almost twelve arduous months.

In relation to Henry, however, who at the time was a newly-wed and had a terribly concerned young wife back in troubled England, the moral issues are far more taxing. Consequently, the real dilemma as to whether or not Henry should have returned to England in order to recuperate still remains unresolved. And the jury quite understandably remains out!

CHAPTER FOUR

Safe and Home Alone

ACT I

'Mr. Amery has asked me to say in reply to your letter of the 4th December about Mrs. Stirling, who is anxious to join her husband in India, that owing to the lack of shipping space to India it has been necessary to impose a general ban on passages to India for the wives of service personnel in that country. Before this ban was imposed there was already a waiting list of some hundreds of persons who had been unable to obtain passages, some of them very hard cases.'

J. A. K. Harrison, private secretary, India Office,
8 December 1942

Once back in the orderly and tranquil Kashmir, without any tiresome emphasis upon duty to the Crown or any immediate commitment to his faraway bride, who as it happens was desperately trying to trace her misplaced husband, Henry began to make preparations for his future. The episode in North Africa in various ways had left its mark, in particular a stark realisation of just how easily he could have been killed. The grim and bloody outcome of action had also dispelled any earlier misrepresentations of war, especially of its so called glamour and of its glory. What was equally telling was that, finally, Henry could now identify the reasons why his parents had been so extremely saddened by his indecent keenness to enlist, to 'bite the bullet'. Knowing that his loving parents had acted in his best interest, within the limits and restrictions imposed on him, he visualised a more carefree lifestyle. For the moment,

India was once again his rightful home. And as soon as he was fit and well, polo, augmented by shooting and fly-fishing, would provide good therapy for the ensuing hot days of recuperation! Sport, though, was not his sole ambition. Having agreed upon an uneasy entente cordiale with his mother, who obviously knew that at some forthcoming period she would most certainly have to accept and help her son to re-establish his studies and marriage, Henry took the decision to discard the Celtic wearing of woad for a lifestyle of *carpe diem* – enjoying the moment, living for the day. A renaissance of past joie de vivre would go some way to remove any unpleasant memories of the grim era of North Africa and of its traumatic aftermath. Meanwhile his love of fishing would flourish, escalating from being a pleasurable pastime to an intense and fervent passion, becoming a most justifiable reason for living. All other childhood hobbies, apart from the climbing of trees that he had once so enjoyed, were now whims of the past: *Fun, Flies and Laughter* had begun.

However, Henry's controversial return to the relative calm and peace of India has somewhat inevitably been the subject of much vivid supposition and quizzical scrutiny. And without wishing to cast further aspersions or possibly add to a clandestine list of valid objections, it nevertheless seems utterly incredible that such a privileged way of life was still readily available to those in the know. The situation becomes even more astonishing when one considers that, all the while Henry was able to pass the time away fishing and occasionally shooting game, the world at large was almost haemorrhaging from the ravages of war.

However eccentric and unwarranted these circumstances may first appear, in order to prevent any further misunderstanding it is perhaps necessary to reiterate Henry's past gallantry, particularly during the autumn of 1939. Indeed, Henry's somewhat resigned and disdainful post-war attitude, which may well have offended a few unapprised friends and foes alike, is more than adequately tempered by his robust stance during that fateful September. Within days of war being declared, with his passionate belief in justice and a healthy appetite for action, without any thoughts of indemnity or financial reward, and while still comparatively safe from imminent call-up, he had immediately volunteered for active service. More than this, he had willingly abandoned a studious and sedate way of life at Peterhouse, which had become a vocation much more in keeping with his casual manner and custom, and had re-entered

Henry's idea of physiotherapy!

Holding the evening supper – note the adverse effects of combat and inactivity – aging and weight gain!

the disciplined and restrictive lifestyle of his past. Thereafter, he had worked tirelessly in his role as lieutenant, Royal Artillery, and as a direct consequence of having faced the might of the magnificent Rommel he had sustained a serious leg wound. And, to cap this misfortune, Henry had developed a painful and irritating kidney condition. This was a reasonably serious medical problem, which would finally end Henry's military career, and his predicament would annoy him immensely up until his eventual return to England, whereupon he was able to receive a course of intense remedial treatment.

During a period of much uncertainty and supposition, clarification of the circumstances arise from a letter dated 15 November 1944. Sent to his mother, Blanche, by staff of the British Military Hospital, Rawalpindi, its politely drafted and rather intimate content is most revealing:

Dear Mrs Stirling,

Your letter of the 12th arrived last evening. The findings of the Medical Board held on your boy here on the 18/4/44 were; that he is suffering from Infected Hydronephrosis of uncertain origin. – The board agree with the recommendation of the medical specialist – and find that Mr Stirling is unfit for any form of military service.

Whereas a touch of drama remains firmly entrenched in any ensuing argument over Henry's true fitness, all in all these unusual circumstances are not comparable to the actions of a cowardly, degenerate idler. In spite of this, however, the scarcity of additional anecdotal evidence makes the unfolding of this less than auspicious period regrettably sketchy, and, in conclusion, reliant upon some imaginative and amusing speculation. Luckily, though, the eloquent Henry who was completely disinterested in maintaining personal diaries, was far keener to record and log his numerous hunting exploits. He was obviously thinking ahead of himself, believing that in his later years he would be able to look back with a great deal of satisfaction over what he had once achieved. As one would expect, however, complications still arise, and, although it is a curious and a highly intriguing experience to study these entries, many of which were written over sixty years ago, several records have faded and are now extremely difficult to decipher. Others, rather sadly, are now completely illegible. In spite of this, there remain numerous entries within a 1943 (fishing and shooting) diary that have survived the inevitable foxing and bleaching that occurs with age, and, apart from some guesswork over the correct spelling of several locations, they help to provide an insight into Henry's exceptional lifestyle. There would be, however, little point in recounting a few of the more successful events of that year without first presenting a short précis of the highly challenging sport, and describing a very odd formula by which the weight of a catch can be calculated.

TO CALCULATE THE WEIGHT OF FISH

The cube of a fish's length gives his weight in lb: it is a rough and ready method, but it is near enough. Here is the formula:– Length plus one-third length multiplied by the square of the girth, and divided by 1,000. As thus, with a fish of 40 inches in length and a girth of 20 inches, it works out as follows:–

$$40 \text{ plus } 13 \text{ (excluding fractions)} = 53$$
$$20^2 = 400$$
$$53 \times 400 = 21,200 \text{ divided by } 1,000 \text{ (excluding fractions)} = 27$$

Weight of the fish is 21 lbs.

This equation was pasted onto the inside rear cover of Henry's 1948 fishing diary.

Robert Traver – the pseudonym of the author, John D. Voelker (1903–1991), an American lawyer who wrote several books on the art of fly-fishing – said, "Fly-fishing is such great fun, I have often felt, that it really ought to be done in bed."

Although very often referred to as another minimalist sport, fly-fishing is a pastime that can become as complex and confusing as one can wish to make it. Henry always kept his fishing matters as simple as possible, making do with his ability to interact with nature and his vast understanding of the broad ecology of a river or lake. As a qualified botanist, a part-time ornithologist and meteorologist all wrapped up in one man, any glimpse of a particular bird or plant was so much more than a pleasing spectacle to the eye; it was unquestionably a passport to success, enabling him to select the right fly for the right location and the correct conditions.

Yet what is fly-fishing? If asked, Henry would invariably answer the simple question in the same straightforward manner:

'Catching one's own supper makes for an ideal ending to the day,

yet in order to do so, the fish caught are killed. So first and foremost as far as I am concerned it is a game sport, otherwise I can see little purpose in the endeavour. Beforehand, however, it entails what the sport suggests, fly-fishing. A form of fishing where you attract and land fish by casting a man-made fly as opposed to casting weighted bait.'

This perfectly reasonable hunting summary of the sport, although unsophisticated, does tend to oversimplify what exactly is involved, thus making any claim that the sport is easily mastered a very grave distortion of the truth. To their peril, many beginners, especially on their first attempt at casting, find themselves entangled in line, and then to their utter dismay the whole process is repeated as they try again. Without question, casting an almost weightless fly is an extremely difficult manoeuvre and, unless a newcomer to the sport has been blessed as a natural, some instruction is usually required. In essence, fly-fishing entails a little more than Henry's short synopsis – an appraisal probably grown from the wealth of experience he had gleaned since childhood. Despite his modesty, unless you are a sporting genius, casting requires constant attention to detail, especially the handling of the rather bulky line which acts as weight. It must be cast and skilfully unrolled in the air whilst delivering the feathery fly to a distant and unsuspecting fish. Whatever else may be made of the sport, it is the act and skill in casting that makes fly-fishing as difficult as it is elegant. In spite of there being several alternative methods of fishing, all of which are in many ways easier, it seems that to dedicated followers none can be anywhere near as satisfying.

Anglers generally agree that engaging the natural world of fly-fishing using a minimum amount of equipment tends to lean towards the select or the very top of their hugely popular sport, while fishing with weight, float and worm bait is usually regarded as being the challenge of the vast majority including the more junior enthusiasts and beginners. Running parallel with this highly acclaimed status, however, comes a form of fishing etiquette similar to the rules that are associated with golf where manners and protocol are of paramount importance. With more and more people now being able to afford and enjoy the art, in order to preserve the standing of the sport, good traditional fly-fishing manners have become not only preferable but essential. Above all, fly-men should respect their fellow anglers by not splashing about their beats, scaring fish and ruining the calm tranquillity that is necessary for success. Additionally, the discovery of a good beat should always be kept a secret between the craftsman, his instinct and his trusted rod. And finally they should remember and strictly adhere to their *Fisherman's Prayer* – by not continually bragging or uttering untruths!

(The art of casting is fully illustrated in the appendix. There is also a glossary to enable the beginner to understand several of the sport's more unusual and oblique terms.)

DIARY 1943
(Adapted 1942 diary, produced by Shalebhoy Tyebjee Sons, Shale Building, Bombay, India.)

January 3
Jakat Sagar (lake). 6 fish: 20 lbs.

January 8
Rode out to hill beyond Temple Bells. Chased two hares near Fox Hole, both of which went to ground. Killed a hare at small hill and a fox on way home. Also 2 small grouse.

January 10
Went out on Delhi Road. Stopped on hill at Mile 14. Saw several packs of big grouse settle on path to left of road. Shot 14. Went onto river and back to left side of road and got 1 snipe. Saw a flock of koonj [cranes]. Bagged 13 big grouse and 1 snipe.

January 17
3 fish: 9 lbs.

January 26–January 30
Several entries showing kills to duck, quail and snipe.
January's success apart from fish killed includes 16 small grouse, 11 snipe, 7 quail, 6 hares, 4 geese, 4 duck, 1 teal and other kills amounting to 77.

February 9
Went to Kailama [?] in morning. Killed one fish: 3½ lbs. Lost another. Both on split golden spoon.

February 10
Kailama in morning. Rose six fish, killed three: 5, 4½ & 4 lbs. Two on split-tailed golden spoon and one on a copper spoon.

February 27
Bilona. Crossed ford and went to overflow. Shot two small grouse and saw a lot of duck. Killed 3 snipe and 2 painted snipe on small marsh below tank. Went up to main tank and waited by well for geese. Got a right and left. Total: 3 snipe, 2 painted snipe, 2 geese and 2 small grouse.

March 7
Jakat Sagar. 6 fish: 18 lbs.

March 12,13,14
Bilona. Total for 3½ days: 26 snipe, 10 geese, 2 teal, 2 hares, 4 duck, 1 small grouse, 3 teter (partridge) and 1 painted snipe.

March 22
Kailama. Fish moving quite well all morning. Killed nine weighing 32 lbs. Best: 6 lbs. All got on copper spoon, which was lost in fish.

Various venues during season including an interesting entry dated April 20:

'Snow water coming down all day. Got nothing in morning. Killed a fish on minnow in afternoon in bridge pool and another in evening in camp pool. Rained at night.'

September 25, 26
Total for two days fishing at Sind Wozil: 20 trout: 19 lbs 14 oz. Best: 2 lbs 5 oz.

Total for season's fishing in Kashmir
510 trout weighing 345 lbs 9 oz. Best: 2 lbs 8 oz (peacock).
Best individual day: 8 trout: 10 lbs 13 oz in Sind Wozil (7 on minnow).

Total fishing for 1942–1943 on Kailama and Jakat Sagar
287 manrial [?]: 983 lbs. Best fish: 10 lbs x 3. About 500 lbs of fish returned.

Total shikar [kill?] for season 1942–43 in Jodhpur
With his father:
371 small grouse, 141 partridge (teter), 72 hares, 52 snipe, 50 quail, 33 big grouse, 24 geese, 14 duck, 10 teal, 10 kooniz, 7 painted [rock?] grouse and 4 painted snipe.

Killed by their dogs:
1 clink [?], 3 hares, 3 teter, 2 foxes and 10 pigeons, 1 wild cat and 1 hawk. Total 803.

Self:
221 small grouse, 100 teter, 46 hares, 45 quail, 41 snipe, 30 big grouse, 15 geese, 9 kooniz, 8 duck, 7 painted grouse, 4 painted snipe and 2 teal.
Total 528 + 10 pigeons.

ACT II

'Mr. Amery regrets therefore that there is very little prospect of his being able to assist Mrs. Stirling but if you wish the case to be pursued further he would be grateful if you could let him know the initials and unit of her husband, whom it has not been able to identify. If he belongs to the British Army, as distinct from the Indian Army, the question of a passage for Mrs. Stirling would in fact be for the War Office to deal with.'
J. A. K. Harrison, private secretary, 8 December 1942

All the while, Henry, in spite of a troublesome knee and a delicate renal condition, was enjoying his rediscovered mercurial childhood, riding, shooting and fishing in picturesque Kashmir, the young Mrs Betty Stirling was toiling away in Britain's bomb-stricken capital. Although there is little evidence to substantiate the claim, it is more than likely that, in addition to a society that was rapidly developing a real sense of egalitarianism, the four years of married solitude that followed Henry's posting to North Africa helped to transform the vulnerable and very traumatised Betty into a truly exceptional and freethinking woman. She possessed not only the culture and intellect associated with the status of being an English rose, but also the down-to-earth and very practical ways of a hard-working factory hand who needed to fend for herself. An instance of how Betty adapted to the hardships of the period was once highlighted by her recollection of using an old pram to gather winter fuel from a local coal merchant. Other examples of her fuel economy are not boiling the kettle more than necessary, saving the tea leaves so that they could be used again, and banking up the fire, which was not lit until it was really essential to do so.

Tips on energy saving, and the welcome 'social insurance' changes radically outlined within the far-reaching Beveridge Report, were not, however, anywhere near Betty's main prerequisite during those tough and troubled winter months of

1942; what was really required was some verifiable idea of the whereabouts of her missing husband.[2] Not being satisfied with the knowledge that Henry had recovered from his leg wound and had been whisked away by his mother to India, she began to write a series of letters to Mr Leo S. Amery, Secretary of State for India and Burma at the Indian Office, SW1, requesting more detailed information about her will-o'-the-wisp, Henry. As a matter of interest, the outspoken Amery was one of the few in Churchill's Cabinet that freely spoke his mind. As a consequence he and Churchill often clashed in relation to India, resulting in Amery once telling the very great man not to speak such nonsense.

After immense delay and several false hopes, Betty slowly began to realise that her search for news was faltering within a state of dire confusion and appalling muddle, and with it any chance of a quick reconciliation. Much to everyone's utter amazement, and to Betty's very understandable annoyance, it appears that not even Mr Amery could shed any further light on the matter, for, officially at least, 2nd Lieutenant Henry Stirling had curiously vanished!

In spite of her husband's untimely disappearance, Betty was not a woman to simply drift from one enterprise to another as if without purpose. With problems multiplying daily she considered that the most appropriate course of action would be that she should work as hard and as diligently as possible for her employer, the British Broadcasting Corporation. Betty's gritty determination that she should *also serve* eventually gained the recognition that her sterling efforts truly deserved, and by 1945 she was appointed on promotion to the position of private secretary to the company's extremely well-known presentation director, John D. M. Snagge, OBE. A career broadcaster since graduation, John's generously warm and refined voice had helped soothe the turbulent airwaves, and had provided the corporation's worldwide audience with a calm steadfast reassurance that all was well.

Such was Betty's admiration for John, and her past standing within the old establishment, that on Wednesday, 15 May 1996 at All Souls Church, Langham Place, London, W1 she was invited to attend a service of thanksgiving for the life and work of this special man, who incidentally also enjoyed the art of fishing.

JOHN SNAGGE, OBE

The voice that tolled the nation's gravest hours
When Britain, girdling fresh from late onslaught,
Was gathering force from springs of vigour fraught
By poisons burst from bombs of evil powers.

The voice that timed the bowman's pendulum,
And gave a meaning count to all those strokes,
While bodies bent and stretched like ladder spokes,
Eyes fixed, ears harking cox as speculum.

For fifty years a man of great event,
For rest his zest for play with rod and line
In weathers hot or cold, careworn or fine,
His happiest hours in flirt with fish were spent.

Not one to brag but always fly the flag,
Our man at helm of History, John Snagge.

Max Robertson, 1 April 1996[3]

Fortunately for Betty, her quite understandable frustration was to be short-lived as contact with her errant husband was eventually achieved. All the same, as the years passed and Henry had graciously extended more consideration by writing more frequently, the challenging distances that any letter would need to overcome made for very hard going. What was equally difficult was that, although a perplexed Betty was now able to draw upon the reassuring news that her wounded officer had been spared from capture and was making good progress back to full health, she remained so very far away from enjoying the comforts of having a husband close at hand.

Betty's extremely sad and sorry situation was also recognised by her understanding and loving grandmother, who in a letter of encouragement wrote the following compassionate words. As a matter of interest, it seems rather likely that Betty's caring and optimistic grandmother may well have been inspired by the consoling lyrics of the hugely popular wartime song 'We'll Meet Again', sung by the immortal Vera Lynn – an obvious analogy being the hopeful prediction of better times and sunnier days ahead.

> *Wellcroft, Caverswall Lane,*
> *Blythe Bridge, Stoke-on-Trent.*
> *Sept 17 1942.*

My Dear Betty

I hope by this time that you are feeling much better and taking care of yourself and that news of Henry is more hopeful, bless you, try to look on the bright side of life and keep cheerful and well ready to meet Henry when the time comes, as it surely will. Things look black now but the sun will surely shine again soon and all will be well. Much love to you all, especially to your dear self.

Yours affectionately,
Granny.

Apart from being home alone, another rather bewildering situation for Betty had existed, for although Henry had been invalided out of the army it seems that there was still utter confusion when and where this had officially occurred. Adding to obvious muddle and more confusion are the uncertainty of certified records, which all appear particularly scant. On reflection, however, perhaps Betty's upsetting dilemma was not so surprising, especially if one appreciates that the problems caused by the notorious fog of war were not solely prescriptive or confined to combat conditions but embraced the whole spectrum of both military and civilian life. Indeed, Betty's circumstances, while subjectively very distressing and somewhat annoying, also need to be placed into these more objective terms: From 3 September 1939 to the end of February 1945 (a total of 66 months) the armed forces of the British Commonwealth and Empire suffered 1,128,315 casualties, a figure that included 307,201 deaths. Civilian losses caused by the enemy bombardment of Britain during the same period totalled 60,585 killed and 86,175 seriously injured. In addition, it was estimated that upward of 150,000 people had suffered slight injuries.[3]

Even apart from this, there can be little doubt that Betty's abandonment and the hurtful culmination of those very questionable events were nevertheless profoundly disturbing, especially the underhandedness of Henry's removal from Cairo to India, which in itself was no mean achievement. What was also very apparent was that the sheer indifference shown by Henry's overprotective parents had caused a very deep and permanent rift principally between Betty and her extremely manipulative mother-in-law.

'Henry's father (Grandpa) was a great favourite of your mother's – loved him to bits but not Mama. I think she was too powerful and selfish. But what a woman! After Henry was injured in the Middle East your Grandmother who knew people in high places had him shipped off to India where he had a high old time!'

Betty Buchanan

Funnily enough, however, and as sure as time tends to ease the pain and hurt of the past, a more forgiving and understanding Betty would always speak very highly of Henry's particularly eccentric parents. Somewhat expectedly, though, any mention of Blanche was usually confined to a short rather terse addendum to a more extensive, warmer appraisal of Henry's father, whom Betty genuinely loved and very much admired. She would frequently describe him as being a kind, considerate, quiet gentleman of the old school – content with life, especially when smoking his pipe while reading and supping an occasional wee dram or two of his favourite Dalmore malt whisky, taken with impunity under the guise of being a therapeutic medicinal nightcap.

CHAPTER FIVE

In the Pink – Out of the Blue!

ACT I

'Betty was on the underground making her way home from a function at the BBC when suddenly she spotted Henry. Completely by chance and as large as life he had entered the same carriage!'

Dominic McDonnell

Unquestionably, after having endured almost six years of war the whole social fabric of Britain was under considerable pressure and in spite of recorded crime falling, other supposedly less striking statistics were showing quite dramatic increases. Motor accidents during 1943, for example, had caused more deaths than enemy bombing raids, and, although seemingly unpalatable at a time when thousands of young men were gathering to free Nazi-occupied Europe, strike action by disillusioned workers had also increased with three times as many working days lost as in 1938.[1] Another phenomenon was the steep and rapid rise in manual employment among women, drafted en masse into factories or, as in Betty's case, into clerical positions that were still nevertheless directly linked to the war effort. It was the general emancipation of woman during the war years that had enabled Betty to travel daily and alone into London, and thereafter work alongside her male colleagues at the BBC without having to endure too many instances of flippant or bigoted innuendo. One other major factor that helped to maintain communal harmony and encouraged gender co-operation within the workplace was the sheer importance of the Corporation. At the outbreak of the Second World War, wireless broadcasting was not only the most important channel for announcing government information, but also the most significant method of influencing public morale. In contrast to more modern times, the many millions of people who were desperately seeking news were simply unable to switch on to the incredible media coverage now provided by hundreds of television and radio stations. Thus, for its time, the BBC was a godsend. With the wireless set being the focal point of every British home, the Corporation was also a cleverly disguised propaganda tool, able to reach out to a national and international audience. Moreover, the people's Beeb was licensed to broadcast all manner of programmes, ranging from the zany comedy of Tommy Handley (*It's That Man Again*) to Prime Minister Churchill's inspiring rhetoric delivered nightly during the *Nine O'clock News* bulletin. This was an opportunity for the gifted and inspirational leader to denounce Nazism as a virulent plague before announcing a succession of Allied victories glorious achieved by honourable and decent men.

As fate would have it, as a direct consequence of Betty's routine of travelling into London via the crowded Underground system into Oxford Circus, a more than just bizarre incident occurred. An astonishing meeting, which would unexpectedly bring her face to face with her castaway husband, was being unwittingly orchestrated. During the early part of 1945, shortly before the cessation of violence, the ambitious although still rather perplexed Henry decided that it was finally time to continue with both his marriage and his learning and as such expand upon the ethos of *carpe diem*. He would once again put pen to paper and write to his most loyal wife informing her of his decision and of his intended return to England.

Coincidentally, Henry's transfer back to London was one of the recommendations of the medical board back in the November of 1944 – an issue that was also mentioned in the letter dispatched to Henry's general practitioner, his mother!

The bitter-sweet news that Henry would return to the shores of England in order to get well must have really upset the doting Blanche. With her connections she would have been informed enough to know that the War in Europe was rapidly coming to an end and that her son would almost certainly be safe from any rearguard enemy action. What was to upset her the most was the knowledge that, ever since 8 September of that year, German V-2 rockets armed with 1-ton warheads had been regularly falling on London. Nevertheless, with her consent, and it appears her financial assistance, Henry set sail.

British Military Hospital
Rawalpindi 15/11/1944

I am sorry to hear that he has not improved in Kashmir. India as you know is not a suitable country for Renal Cases.
  To my mind he did not look like a Tubercular subject.
  I hope that as a result of transfer to England he will quickly improve.
  Sincerely Yours,
  Col. John Roe

Henry, in spite of his mother's genuine fears for his safety, had also decided upon one other outstanding matter. Once back in his new home and, in some way, a new country, he would reject any offer that would enable him to rejoin the course on mechanical engineering. This had been a second-choice subject, only having been selected on the grounds of it being both practical and suitable. The only subject he would read at university would most definitely be his beloved forestry.

Returning to his wife and finally becoming free from his painful renal problem were not, however, the only reasons why Henry would finally say his farewell to the country of his birth. Knowing how world order was rapidly changing, he feared the worst for his beloved India. He also recognised that along with the more general feelings of disillusionment and civil unrest, which were quickly spreading throughout the country, was British India's demand for total independence. With matters rapidly deteriorating it seemed that every delicate situation or mishap that could possibly be blamed upon colonial rule was; and almost all of the many political gatherings were constantly being inflamed by anti-British proclamations. This fact was made more noticeable by speeches made by the more radical Indian leaders in the mould of Jawaharlal Nehru. Indeed, arrangements for British withdrawal were being so fiercely negotiated that it would ultimately require the King's cousin, Admiral Louis Mountbatten, Viscount

Mountbatten of Burma, to personally intervene and provide calm reassurances to an increasingly hostile Indian population.

Knowing that all was lost for India, especially in relation to his rather old-fashioned view upon colonialism, and realising that for the ruling classes, whether British or otherwise, the country would never be quite be same, Henry still maintained a positive attitude. Regardless of the Indianisation process, and whatever else that may happen in the future, nothing would prevent his pursuit of happiness or hinder his quest for achievement.

For once, Henry's next assignment appeared relatively straightforward bar one insurmountable problem: his need to return to England. With there being no other alternative available Henry also knew that standing against a newly found adventurous spirit was the need to prepare for a most dramatic change of lifestyle and of fortune. His initial requirements were threefold: wife and family support, appropriate medication to clear his renal condition, and lastly the finding of a suitable university. His overall and ultimate goal was also very clear – it would be success. Meanwhile the only significant sting in the tail was his destination, a battle-scarred England, a country he had not visited for almost four highly relevant years, and one which was a very far cry from the increasingly unhappy, unsettled yet nevertheless extremely picturesque British Kashmir.

In total defiance of all statistical odds, it was to be a combination of these unusual circumstances that subsequently brought about their 'out of the blue' and almost unbelievable Underground reunion. The bizarre scenario surrounding the timely assignation is still quite vividly remembered by the couple's close friend, Dominic McDonnell:

'It had been one evening when Betty was on her way home after having attended a social function at the B.B.C. Although she had known that after all those years Henry's long awaited return to England was now more than just wishful thinking on her part, she was still very unsure of any actual date or expected time of arrival. Consequently you can well imagine her feelings – a great deal of shock and complete surprise – especially when she first spotted Henry. Even more so, as Henry casually entered the same carriage acting as if nothing to cause any unease had happened, and as though he had never strayed from his duty or had been away from her side. Knowing Henry as I do, he most probably

joked and made light of the moment before he cheekily and rather accusingly began to question Betty, outrageously asking her where she had been and where she was heading. Then with that laugh of his, he no doubt began to charm and smooth his way round this extremely awkward almost surreal situation. By the time they had eventually completed the journey home, Betty was more than likely feeling very sorry for her gallant soldier husband who had been coerced into withstanding all manner of beastly conditions, first imposed upon him by the army, then the wretched enemy, and then to cap it all by his annoying and interfering mother, who he once described as a "squat little thing"!'

The knowledge that the couple were safely reunited and that Henry was now gradually regaining his health would have given the Hawleys, at least, a great deal of comfort, especially after so many years of uncertainty. Nevertheless there were many differences to put right, particularly how Henry would manage to cope with matters without having any immediate prospects of a job or a guaranteed place at a suitable university. Another significant problem that Henry needed to overcome was just how he would adjust to married life and all the responsibilities and compromises that the status entailed.

Given that the ambitious Henry obviously required some form of qualification to eventually succeed, it seems that under all the circumstances it somewhat justifiably fell upon his parents to keep to their promise of offering some additional help.

Henry for his part attuned extremely well to having Betty at his side, and as a result quickly buckled down to the virtues of married life. Almost immediately he not only secured some temporary clerical work, but had also taken another momentous step into the unknown by becoming a parent in his own right.

Their first child, Jennifer, was born on 27 January 1946. The loving and loyal Betty dutifully left her position with the BBC to become a full-time mother – almost the universal practice for married women at the time. Meanwhile, Henry, as to be expected, treated this miraculous outcome as an ideal opportunity to seek further adventure. He performed yet another amazing volte-face by sending off an application form to a dark-blue university, the progressive St Catherine's College, Oxford.[2]

ACT II

'This is to certify that from my personal knowledge of H. H. D. Stirling I have full confidence in recommending him for acceptance of S. Catherine's Society, Oxford: his record at Downside School was excellent, and I was the Headmaster for the period concerned.'

C. A. Rutherford, Worth Priory, Crawley, Sussex,
9 April 1946

In retrospect, Henry's decision to once again leave his wife and on this occasion a young child appears quite remarkable. Although the separation was not expected to be for very long, the words utterly complacent and eminently selfish come immediately to mind. Yet in fairness the particularly difficult rather cruel decision was not made in order to increase his self-importance, nor was it made to fuel any confident alter ego. To Henry, acceptance into St Catherine's would simply comply with the next stage of his well-planned overall strategy for securing future happiness for his newly found family. Perhaps what was even more relevant was that the college, known affectionately as St Catz with its motto *Nova et Vetera* (the new and the old) afforded grants to successful applicants.[3]

As a starting point, Henry's first requirement was to secure a corroborative testimony to that of his former head teacher at Downside. On 29 March of that year the deputy lieutenant and justice of the peace for Somerset, Lieutenant Colonel Hartley Maud (retired), answered Henry's prayers:

'I have known Henry Stirling for a considerable number of years. He is, to the best of my belief, a gentleman of honesty, sobriety and integrity, who has been wounded when serving as an officer with His Majesty's Forces.'

To understand the true significance of Henry's entry into St Catherine's, one must remember how very much matters had changed after the war, not only for the country as a whole but in particular for Henry. There were several substantial differences. He was now to be a mature student with a wife and young child, he was renting accommodation in Finchley and supporting his family by way of temporary office work, and what was more taxing was that he faced the growing problem of having the challenge of greater competition than ever before. There was another worrying impasse to overcome: his persistent and very often painful kidney infection, which had become so troublesome that when Henry finally managed to secure his place at the college, he was required to write his letter of thanks to St Catherine's from a local hospital bed. The summer and early autumn of 1946 were indeed difficult weeks for the usually carefree Henry.

In spite of these worries and the stresses that they inevitably caused, Henry Stirling succeeded in achieving what most scholars would deem impossible. On 11 October, six months after his application, Henry matriculated into the darker shade of blue of Oxford after having earlier worn the lighter blue of Cambridge.

The assistant registrar, S. Caldwell, completed entry 2137 of the University Register by certifying:

On the above date a Certificate was registered by Mr. H. H. D. Stirling (St Catherine's Society) exempting him from responsions.

Commencing his studies in the Michaelmas term, 1946, Henry was blessed with further good fortune. The course proposed was to be a complete joy.

Course proposed: Honours Moderations in Geology and Botany, 4 Term Course. Then 5 Terms Forestry.

Lectures	Tuesday	Wednesday	Thursday	Friday	Saturday
9	Mensuration	–	Forest Management	–	
10	Geology	Botany	Geology	Geology	–
11	Geology	Botany	Geology	Geology	–
12	Geology	Botany	Geology	Geology	Geology*
2	–	Botany Lecture	–	Botany	–
3	–	Botany Labs	–	Botany	–
4	Botany	Botany Labs	–	Botany	–
5	Botany	Botany Labs	Geology	Geology	–
6	–	Botany Labs	Geology	Geology	

* Every 2nd week

Botany – Miss Trevaldwyne.
Geology – Mr Bazzard.[4]

From the outset an excited Henry acted as if the world had been through a cleverly programmed period of suspension, as though the past six years of war-torn strife had somehow not existed. He was back at another college of excellence and, apart from his passion for fly-fishing, he was doing what he enjoyed most – mixing sport and fun with light-hearted academia. The fair city of Oxford would soon learn of Henry and of his eccentricities, and furthermore his laughter and boisterousness would also attract several like-minded souls, all of whom were hell bent on once again enjoying life. Not even Betty's eventual move into rented accommodation in Oxford would deter the married Henry from pursuing fun. Before expanding upon Henry's time at St Catherine's, however, some measure should be given to the unsuspecting college and its unique and progressive origin. It was founded on an "initiative by which the University sought to open itself to a much larger and poorer class. For centuries one of the fundamental requirements for entry to Oxford had been residence in a college or hall. The considerable expense of living within a college was, however, a bar to many students who were otherwise entirely able to meet the academic requirements. The passage of the Education Act in 1944 coupled with post-war introduction of grants, guaranteed financial support for any student accepted by the University."[5]

Convinced that he had little to fear from further study, and determined to combine work with pleasure, Henry, who could suitably impress fellow students by speaking virtually fluent Latin, and who could rouse amusement by uttering risqué Hindi, quickly made friends. As usual, however, these companions were not run-of-the-mill characters of mediocrity – far from it. One such friend, Ralph Farrer, was particularly well connected in pre- and post-war society, having an aunt who had married Sir Oswald Ernald Mosley, the tempestuous politician who had abandoned his chance of being the next Labour prime minister by resigning and becoming leader of the British Union of Fascists.

'I was thinking of Henry only a few days ago when Shirley and I bought a 17-acre farmlet on which to grow a forest. I imagined his reaction: "What's that old fool Geoff starting a forest for at his time of life?" or something like that, with that familiar barking laugh of his.

'Then your letter took me back to Oxford in 1946 when I first met Henry. I wasn't quite sure what I had met. What vigour! What

ribaldry! How was it that Henry, along with that zany and sardonic Australian Jock Bryce, and gentlemanly Ralph Farrer, came to be my friends I don't know. We were a motley crew on the face of it. Ralph's mother was one of the anarchical Mitfords, so there could have been a wild streak in him too. As for me, I was a tentative, even nervous sort of chap, and indeed I was asked by the more holy scholards, on several occasions, how I could possibly associate myself with such a gang of rambunctious rebels.

'After so long in the forces, I suppose we all needed to let off steam, and I think now that Henry and the others kept me sane by being a bit mad.

'What a man he was! Under that spiky and crusty exterior there lurked a tender soul, I'm sure. I shall never forget that laugh. And I always relished the fierce arguments we had, and shall continue to enjoy the memory of them.'

Shirley and Geoffrey Chavasse, Rotorua, New Zealand

Inevitably, Henry's quest for fun and laughter eventually began to take its toll academically, and although initial reports on his studies revealed exceptional keenness those following began to disclose an adverse degree of complacency. Henry's forestry tutor and overall course mentor, Mr William Day, noted this growing boisterousness on more than the one occasion.

St. Catherine's Society, Oxford.

Report for: Forestry   *Term: 1949*
Name: H. H. D. Stirling   *Subject: Forestry*

He has taken no tutorials this term, but reports regarding his other work are, on the whole, satisfactory. A certain lightness (and noisiness) of spirit seems to have been responsible for some unfavourable opinion but it would appear that he should do reasonably well.

W. R. Day

Please return to the Censor during the seventh week of term. Statement of fees payable should be sent at once.[6]

Several months later in the summer of 1949, Henry's failure to study with consistency and focused attention to detail brought about an unnecessary stream of hesitation and in addition a fair amount of self-inflicted worry. Henry, much to his surprise, was only to achieve third-class honours in forestry. Yet, even this unexpected development was quickly overcome in a familiar manner. Having bid his farewells to St Catherine's, Henry faced another unexpected hurdle. While he would have preferred to take a year out in order to rekindle his passion for fishing, circumstances called for action. What was urgently required was a sound career in a reputable company, and a position where there was scope for promotion and thus greater remuneration. With all his skill and ability to outmanoeuvre life's difficulties, he quickly sought the support of his large circle of contacts and close friends.

Telephone No. 3527   *St. Catherine's Society,*
Oxford
1. X. 49

Mr H. H. D. Stirling matricated in the University of Oxford as a member of St Catherine's Society in October 1946 and was in residence till June 1949 reading for the Honours School of Forestry. In this he was placed in the Third Class – a completely unexpected result. All the reports of his various Tutors had really pointed to a higher class and that is my own personal impression of his abilities.

For he is, undoubtedly, a really intelligent man, quick, keen, hard-working. He is, moreover, well educated in the widest sense, with many interests. He is a ready conversationalist and a pleasant companion and a man to be thoroughly trusted in every way. I am sure that in any post he would prove to be reliable, really alive and enterprising, a pleasant and welcome associate and a thoroughly reliable and intelligent worker.

V. J. K. Brook, Censor [7]

ACT III

'To whom it may concern:
'I have known Henry Stirling for over fifteen years. I can safely say and honestly state that he is a man of excellent character and sound principles. He is the kind of person who will carry out efficiently and conscientiously whatever task that may be allocated

99

to him and who will spare no pains to achieve the best result. He possesses a brighter-than-average intelligence, and is one of those many thousands of men whose studies were interrupted by the war; he was nevertheless able, while bearing the responsibilities of married life, to apply himself with vigour to his studies at Oxford, and to gain his Bachelor's degree in Forestry, with 3rd Class Honours – no easy task even in the most favourable circumstances. I can heartily recommend him to any employer who is lucky enough to receive an offer of his services. '

**Clerk of the Bank of England, Palace Gate, London,
26 September 1949**

Within the year, and after having secured two magnificent testimonies from successful networking, Henry found a position that he considered ideal. It offered him stability and, if he managed to play his cards correctly, an opportunity to travel; he applied for the post of assisted technical officer for the Deciduous Fruit Board, Garrick Street, London, WC2. In the meanwhile Henry had hopes of further success, for he rejoined his family and also secured his own home. Moreover he was soon to meet some rather interesting neighbours – in particular, Luis Gabriel Portillo.

With the benefit of hindsight, the very idea of an unassuming yet dogged Spanish Socialist Republican and a boisterous British right-of-centre Conservative becoming neighbours and friends seems extraordinarily bizarre. According to the wonderfully liberal-minded and charming Cora Portillo, Franco's Spain and the country's recent civil war was probably not a subject on which Henry would have had much knowledge, yet as practising Catholics devoted to Christian values they were obviously united in their loathing of totalitarian dictatorships. This was particularly true of the disgusting method of mirroring the many eschatological and liturgical attributes of the churches, while being fundamentally hostile towards them. Mussolini and General Franco were prime examples: they enjoyed flirting with the papacy in order to appear supposedly righteous.

Parallel with their disapproval of ultra-right regimes were other essential elements that brought them closer: their love of family life, especially the gift of children; their immense intellect; and the fact that brutal war had once shattered their careers. Luis, after having learnt English, had like Betty worked for a while at the

BBC. He was most certainly more than a match for Henry academically, becoming a doctor of law at an early age, a professor of civil law at Salamanca University and a gifted writer. Luis, again in keeping with his Conservative neighbour, was a fighter, a Don Quixote, willing to right the wrongs and injustices of this often cruel life. In equal measure they were two rather eccentric gentleman of the old school who thoroughly enjoyed what they saw as a duty: to charm the ladies by their amazing and eloquent vocabulary – Henry with his teasing and warm smile, Luis with his idealism and his gallant kissing of their hands. When together in the same room, the sound of fun and laughter would soon echo around any household, children either being whisked around inside Henry's large fishing waders, or sitting spellbound by Luis's mesmerising ability to cut paper silhouettes of animals. It is little wonder that Luis was asked and subsequently agreed to be godfather to Henry's youngest daughter.

Having a charming Spanish romantic as a neighbour may well be considered out of the ordinary, yet another of Henry's most striking and interesting neighbours was a Mrs Myra Hindley! Not the infamous lover of the Moors Murderer Brady, but a husky-voiced Jewish communist and divorcee who lived two doors down. Funnily enough, it appears that so long as politics were not mentioned or discussed with any vigour Henry and Myra got on rather well. However, what was more likely was Betty's tactful and timely intervention, which kept good order and neighbourly tranquillity. Over the ensuing years, especially at social gatherings, one can well imagine the intrigue of friends as both Betty and the mischievous Henry revelled in delightful yet rather macabre innuendo and name-dropping. Many unsuspecting guests would visibly step a yard or so closer to Henry as he would dramatically and cleverly use the anomaly by reminiscing about his past friendship with that woman! However, after a minute or so of harmless teasing, and to avoid any additional misunderstanding, the truth was eventually revealed, followed by a huge roar of laughter.

Few revellers at Henry's frequent parties would have realised the true extent of Henry's vast network of friends. Many held prominent positions in the City, in law and, above all, in medicine. Whereas Henry held each and every one of their friendships extremely dear, one unique character in the field of psychiatry comes to mind – Dr Michael Raymond, Fellow of the Royal College of

Physicians and a Fellow of the Royal Society of Medicine, a rare honour for a psychiatrist. Indeed, many family members often recall the intensity of their discussions relating to the hidden and very often unmentionable illness. Michael, a rugby chum from the Minehead days, was particularly fascinating, and, like Luis Portillo, he could adequately hold his own with Henry's wit during any intellectual discussion. Henry, who in spite of fully understanding the importance of pioneering work into sexual deviancy, purposely remained highly sceptical of Michael's highly acclaimed investigation into fetishism.[8] So typical of Henry, the subject simply provided too much scope for comic banter – particularly stories of men obsessed with ladies' handbags and perambulators! Inevitably, however, Michael's charm and wonderful fishing company overcame Henry's light-hearted flippancy, and yet another very strong bond of friendship was formed.

CHAPTER SIX

The Peach-Tasting Marketing Detective!

ACT I

'With reference to our discussion this morning. I am writing to confirm your appointment as Assistant Technical Officer of the London Office of the Deciduous Fruit Board, at a commencing salary of £400 per annum, inclusive, as from 1st February, 1950. The appointment is subject to termination by one month's notice on either side. Third-class travelling expenses and hotel expenses when absent from London on official business will be reimbursed to you. I shall be glad if you will be good enough to acknowledge receipt of this letter.'

G M. Dykes, Deciduous Fruit Board, Garrick Street, London

Few who have experienced the responsibilities of becoming a father and sole provider for a young family in post-war Britain are likely to deny that Henry at last appeared to have grasped reality. Whatever may have occurred earlier, particularly within his extraordinary marriage, could not in any way refute a welcome and newly found maturity. No longer able to escape the burdens that frequently mirror the joys of parenthood by following an avant-garde lifestyle, Henry needed to toil. Any idealistic dream of having a wonderful home and family, which would be able to live and holiday in comparative comfort, required the security of a well-remunerated position. For a while at least, it appears that Henry, the fisherman who always considered talk of money vulgar, would need to curtail his lifelong passion and fully concentrate on earning a salary.

With a ruthless determination to succeed, which probably helped to overcome a great deal of uncertainty, Henry quickly sent a letter of acceptance confirming his appointment as a technical biologist with the Deciduous Fruit Board. Their premises in Garrick Street, in the very heart of London, had the truly splendid-sounding telephone number, Temple Bar 9067.

Facing another fresh challenge, however, immediately caused Henry to ponder a reoccurring dilemma – one that had plagued him throughout his remarkable life – should he behave and act as he had always done, or should he at long last show some dignified restraint?

So, typical of Henry, there was no turning back, and within a few days he was anxiously exploring various avenues of fun. One can only imagine the laughter in the laboratories and warehouses while Henry was busily dissecting and grading various deciduous fruit, and the cheeky double entendre that accompanied his most eloquently delivered terminology of each particular sample. Words such as overripe, well-formed, clean, hand-picked and mature were simply tailor-made. Additional chaos would have no doubt arisen from his deliberate misinterpretations of marketing jargon – phrases and terms such as 'free from injury or damage', 'russeting', 'limbrubs', 'hail and sprayburn', 'broken skin' and 'disease'. For the mischievous Henry there was an abundance of material available to sustain his constant rapport with fun!

It seems that one of Henry's unorthodox skills, based upon laughter and bringing success, was a clever adaptation of an earlier maxim referred to, inasmuch as laughter is the best medicine. Moreover there is a wealth of evidence that this unusual theory not only made him a delight to work alongside and toil with, but also earned him the respect of management. A clear confidence in his own natural ability, and tackling the challenges of work and leisure time with a resolute yet entertaining determination were obvious attributes, clear to all that knew him. As a consequence, Henry was subsequently promoted to marketing director.

Added to Henry's 'whistle while you work' theory was his rather flamboyant dress code – a character trait that would probably annoy and frustrate modern consultants in the art of self-adornment and their equally quirky confidence-building gurus. Henry was not one to be easily fooled by pretentiousness; he knew that looking stylish was as much about knowing what not to wear and that style has little or no bearing on slavishly following fashion. In the sanctuary of his managerial status, Henry was perfectly happy wearing the almost obligatory suit or jacket and very often set a standard by wearing a bow tie. On the other hand, however, when duties entailed a visit to the warehouse, Henry favoured Hush Puppies and a Montgomery-style military duffel coat. The warm, windproof and robust duffel, with its leather toggles and horn pegs, complementing a roomy hood and deep patch pockets, was so much more than an overcoat. In keeping with the bow tie it too made a bold statement as to the status of the wearer.

Looking every inch like Jack Hawkins's gritty portrayal of Captain Ericson from the endangered *Compass Rose* in the magnificent 1950s film *The Cruel Sea*, or alternatively Ian Fleming's dashing 007, James Bond, it seems that the stylish Henry, regardless of how he was dressed, managed to totally captivate his co-employees, including the office cleaners. It also seems very likely that, whether or not Henry was working within the remit of the London boardroom or generally lending a helping hand to the warehouse and distributing staff in Cape Town, he simply refused to allow his particularly lofty position to overshadow the down-to-earth principle of *Fun, Flies and Laughter!*

'I have so many fond memories of the D.F.B. working as Henry's and Norman Sheldon's secretary. So many things remind me of Henry: cayenne pepper, waders, salmon, whisky, hush puppies, green shirts, bow ties . . . . etc, etc! He once left a fresh pear on his desk and left it there until it was dried and shrivelled. He later gave it to me, and I still have it today! (He did the same thing with an orange, I think.)

'On one occasion when Norman Sheldon decided that the offices needed redecorating I was given the job of asking each staff member what colour scheme they would like for their office. Henry insisted he would like a black ceiling! Norman who was unimpressed wouldn't allow it. (Henry got his own back later however when he scuppered the open-plan idea when NG was away in S. Africa.)

'There was another fun time when Henry told our Italian office cleaners how much he liked Italian food. The next evening they duly arrived with a large pasta meal for us (Richard Brighten, Henry, Sandy Bennett and me). We all sat round Henry's desk and enjoyed a lovely meal. They also provided wine, plates, napkins etc.

*Looking every inch like the great Jack Hawkins'
portrayal of Captain Ericson.*

007 Henry together with Q, the resolute Norman Sheldon.

'The memory of Henry's penetrating laugh rising over the hubbub of a crowd is so very true and particularly apt. I could often overhear Henry's laughter from his office across the corridor and his conversations on the phone to the panel salesmen – he was always offering to "take down their particulars" with a chuckle in his voice. It is also very true to read "encounters with Henry were never dull" – I'm sure all those lives he touched can recall their own particular memories of him, it was a real pleasure to have known him.'

Linda Walker, Sidcup, Kent, 30 May 1993

'I never see a duffle coat without thinking of Henry – his was the first I ever saw.'

Mary, Egham, Surrey

'Henry was my principal mentor when I first joined the D.F.B. nearly twenty-five years ago. His style and sense of humour were inspirational and he became a legend in the fruit trade. Working with Henry was never dull. There was always something new on the go and every day a new anecdote. His sense of fun was a boon to team spirit and his eloquence was exemplary.'

Richard (Dick) Brighten, Chingford, London

'My memories of Henry go back to the Garrick Street days and that Dickensian building from which people seemed to "pop-out" from various cubby holes. I particularly recollect a somewhat alcoholic journey around the U.K. with Henry, soon after I joined the D.F.B. – finishing up at a dreadful Victorian-Gothic hotel in Hull, where they started vacuuming the lounge about 10 p.m. In spite of Henry's predilection for fishing I cherish the good times we had together.'

Peter Swinyard, London

'Henry was a very great friend – almost the only member of the D.F.B. staff who was prepared to give me the time of day in the beginning of my nine years with the Board. I remember so well the journeys to Southampton with him and his ready laugh.'

John Lindsay, Dedham, Essex

'1969 was the year when I met Henry for the first time and during our time together at the D.F.B. we established a marvellous *relationship, especially when we had to attend those compulsory fishing trips and the visits to Conferences that usually ended in excesses of all sorts of activities which Henry seemed to be able to handle far better than anyone else.*

'Henry was very much my mentor but also a good friend and he leaves me with a wealth of happy memories that I will always cherish.'

Geoff, Belton-in-Rutland, Leicestershire

'Henry was a great character and those of us who were his colleagues at the old D.F.B. in Garrick Street and later in the Strand remember him with great affection and respect.'

Ron Vollor, Hindhead, Surrey

'Henry was the very first person at the D.F.B. to make me feel welcomed back in England, and the one person there that I could laugh with, and I remember too what a pleasure it was to meet him in Capetown. When Henry came out on one of his visits, Bill and I were feeling a bit fed up and homesick. Henry was like a "gale" of fresh air and cheered us up.'

Muriel and Bill Thompson

In his capacity as marketing director, Henry unquestionably came to benefit from the autonomy and freedom that this position bestowed. Added to these twin advantages was the need for Henry to inspire and motivate his overseas marketing team in South Africa. This delicate and skilful task, which entailed occasional visits to the country's 'mother city' of Cape Town was a complete joy for Henry. He really adored his trips to the Cape and his ventures into the flourishing fruit fields beyond the magnificent setting of the city's national park – a thousand hectares of relatively untainted wilderness dominated by the mighty Table Mountain:

'Today I went to look at some farms. It was really quite incredible to see all these wonderful black women working while actually carrying their children across their backs. The Afrikaners call this abba cradling, and the cloth fastening straps are called tjalies (African? pronounced Charlies) And to see others sitting side by side putting grapes in boxes while their babies lay on the floor underneath. . . . I wish you could be here, you would love the sun and the place.'

Officially recognised in the 1930s as a thriving metropolis, the legislative capital of Cape Town and much of the 75-kilometre (47-mile) stretch of peninsula still represents an impressive blend of modern suburbia adorned by mountain, beach and wooded valleys. With a history of British and Dutch colonialism together with an influx of Indonesian, Malay and African rural immigrants looking for work, Cape Town remains a most fascinating example of flourishing multiculturalism.[1] Indeed, today Robben Island (Robbe Eiland or Seal Island) acts as a modern symbol of Nelson Mandela's and South Africa's long struggle for democracy, with many of its residents and tour guides having been former political prisoners of the past regime.

However, without wishing to dwell on South Africa's troubled political past, the pride of the Cape is undeniably the fertile soil of the bountiful Cape Winelands and, further afield, the fertile orchards of the Western Cape. One of the most important reasons for the development of the Cape's fruit-growing industry was the destructive effect of phylloxera, which threatened to destroy the winegrowers' only source of income. Equally important were the climatic conditions of the area, especially the vast Drakenstein Valley where astute winegrowers quickly began to utilise the fertile soil. This proved to be extremely sympathetic to the growing of all deciduous fruit types: peaches, apples, apricots, table grapes and plums. What is more, even greater good fortune came their way owing to the increase in demand for fresh fruit in Europe. Consequently with an opportunity for export, an explosion within the fruit industry occurred and by the early 1900s the foothills of Paarl (Peerlebergh, Dutch for pearl mountain) and the adjacent lowlands between the Klein Drakenstein and Du Toitskloof mountains annually produced more than 100,000 tons of deciduous fruit, approximately a quarter of the Cape Colony.[2]

As South Africa approached the 20th century other phenomena took place. Once gold and precious stones were discovered, more and more immigrants were eager to make their way to the Cape, aptly named the Gateway to Africa, in order to seek their fortunes in the increasing number of mines and diamond fields. "So it was that on 8 March 1900 the Union-Castle Mail Steamship Co. Ltd. was born."[3] For well over a century this company was to provide an essential mail, cargo and passenger link between the United Kingdom and its glorious dominion of South Africa.

By 1909, the first act of the new chairman, Sir Owen Phillips was to negotiate a fresh mail contract. 'Not only mail would be carried, but produce exported would be charged special rates. Pedigree stock from Europe was to be carried free of charge and, to help the infant fruit industry, 18,000 cubic feet of cold- or cool-chamber space was to be installed in every mailship. The mid-twenties saw the appearance of the first mailship in excess of 20,000 tons – the *Carnarvon Castle*. In addition, she was the first of a long line to be powered by diesel engines.' Almost inevitably, during '1936 the *Stirling Castle* (25,554 tons) made history by accomplishing the voyage from Southampton to Cape Town in 13 days and 9 hours, thus breaking the record set up by the *Scot* (6,844 tons) as far back as 1893'. One can only wonder if the seventeen-year-old Henry Stirling knew of the event and whether or not, subconsciously at least, the *Stirling Castle*'s feat had any bearing upon his future.[4]

As expected, the outbreak of the Second World War and the need for tighter control, together with the unpalatable fact that exporters faced bankruptcy if exports were halted, heralded the requirement of a statutory and controlling body. As a direct result, in the October of that same year the Deciduous Fruit Board was established. Such was the success of the marketing of deciduous fruit that by the 1979/80 seasons a peak of some 261,000 metric tonnes were exported.[5]

Sadly, however, due to rocketing oil prices, the relentless growth of air travel, and the introduction of the elegant Concorde, similar success failed to embrace the Union-Castle Line and its wonderful cruise and shipping fleet. And in spite of an upbeat John Andreae, the Union-Castle's passenger director, during 1976, reminding agents of the breathtaking service his company could provide – joking that "travel by mail ship would never be supersonic but it would always be a super-tonic" – the writing for the wonderful Union-Castle Line was most certainly on the wall.[6] As sure as bad news always tends to travel fast, matters quickly became untenable. By the spring of 1977, due to relentless escalation of operating costs and the switching of cargo to container ships, passenger liners became an unaffordable luxury.

Consequently 'the *Windsor Castle*, the last Union-Castle passenger mailship, returned to Southampton on September 19, 1977 – 120 years and four days after the 530-ton *Dune* sailed down Southampton Water on the first epic voyage to South Africa. It fell to the *Southampton Castle* to make the last ever mailship voyage between the UK and South Africa, and her return to her home port on October 24, 1977 marked the end of a large tradition of service, carrying mail, passengers and cargo on this route.'[7]

SALUTE TO THE CASTLES

Castles are our memories, Castles are our pride,
Sadly now we mark their passing day,
Remembering the tall ships straining on the tide
And bringing up the dawn in Table Bay.
Southward gleam the seaways, seas they knew so well,
Buffeting through Biscay, blistered in the sun;
A long, long line of Castles, dipping in the swell,
To keep the weekly bargain on the great Cape run.
Castles were our calling, Castles were our trade,
Our purpose and our passion and our creed;
They were a part of history whose story will not fade,
Helping to build a continent, serving a nation's need;
The Castles brought the lifeblood, the people and the mails,
The rich, the poor, the restless and the great,
Cotton goods and Paris hats, machines and iron rails,
Eternal as the seasons and hardly ever late.
From Isle of Wight and Durban Bluff, Sea Point and Signal Hill,
Year in, year out they greeted the Castles steaming by,
Each one dear, familiar friend and all remembered still,
For ships and men come and go but honour does not die;
From Windsor to Balmoral, Athlone to Armadale,
Capetown, Kinfauns, Llanstephan, the names ring out like bells;
A hundred years they sailored and did not fault or fail;
Here's a toast to all the proud ships as we say our sad farewells.

K. J. Brett[8]

ACT II

'Princess Margaret surprised BBC Chiefs last night by singing "No you can't chop your Mama up in Massachusetts" when she went to the Television Centre last night Earlier the Princess had gone into the TV Theatre – the old Shepherds Bush Empire – to see "What's my Line?" She was intrigued with one of the

competitors, Mr. Henry Stirling from Stanmore, Middlesex, who is a "peach taster". She laughed and clapped at his mime which he later explained portrayed him taking the temperature of peaches.'

Philip Phillips, *Daily Express*, 7 February 1956

Q uite apart from his wonderful and expenses-paid business trips to Cape Town, other fortuitous benefits that ran parallel with status were those little extras known as the perks of the job. To the party-loving Henry, these bonuses, which were usually comprised of business lunches and evening cocktail parties focusing upon promoting good public relations and a first-class corporate image, were an absolute godsend. Divine providence had once again intervened and could not have selected a more appropriate stage for him to act out and perform his sociable managerial role. With Henry at the helm, the time to set sail and hope for a fair wind was ripe. Displaying a sound knowledge of the product and, with unquestionable ease, a charming almost boyish manner and *fruity* laugh, Henry adored and excelled at such social gatherings. And, in keeping with his father, Henry delighted in sipping cocktails or quality malt as opposed to drinking copious pints of stomach-swelling ale. With the occasional exception, beer, home-made or otherwise, was exactly that, to be drunk at home after arduous toil in the garden. There was, though, one exemption from the rule: the lunch party held at Moor Cottage on New Year's Day. This was an annual event, where assorted beers, wines and black velvet could be enjoyably quaffed to the full. (Black velvet is cold Guinness mixed with either chilled champagne or a good-quality sparkling wine.)

With prospects improving, the canny Henry not only displayed a rare talent as a company botanist, but had also developed a keen eye for the complementary and extremely pleasurable perks within the marketing side of the business. Determined to endorse a policy expounding the power of laughter, Henry actually believed that, in order to achieve success, laughter was an essential ingredient, helping those smiling and chuckling participants improve upon their status and role in life, whether in business or otherwise. With uncommon gusto, he quickly and rather craftily added this tried-and-tested formula to an undeniably shrewd and gifted marketing brain. With his own career prospects in mind, and knowing the irrefutable value of presenting to the world at large a wholesome and equitable corporate image, Henry agreed to be a contestant on

112

Taking the temperature of a South African peach.

the BBC's extremely popular television panel game called *What's My Line?* In spite of the game's trivial vagaries, which required very little skill from the contestants, by 1956 the televised show had attained great success. Indeed, all that was required of the guest contestants was to be perceptive enough to recognise that their particular occupation was exceptionally unusual. Thereafter they simply entered the stage area in front of the panel and signed in; they performed a short mime of the job that they performed, before answering yes or no to a maximum of ten questions put to them by four panellists who were attempting to work out their occupation. Humour and a great deal of Irish charm was added to the programme by the show's talented and agreeable chairman, the Dublin-born former sports commentator, and ex-amateur boxer, Eamonn Andrews.

On 6 February 1956, in the presence of Her Royal Highness Princess Margaret, Henry duly signed in and took to the stage. Within seconds of performing a most peculiar and particularly mystifying mime, the bemused panel and the entire studio audience, including the baffled Princess were beside themselves, with many shrieking in uncontrollable laughter. More to the point, a nationwide television audience was also in stitches; many thousands of viewers were wondering where and to what Mr Henry Stirling had delicately

BBC Television

BBC Television

DIPLOMA

This Parchment certifies that on the night of

6th of February 1956

Mr. Henry Sterling the Peach Taster

"Beat the Panel" in **"What's my Line?"**

at the

BBC Studios, Lime Grove, London

The Panel

Chairman

Producer

The incorrect spelling of Henry's surname would have unquestionably angered the unaware and grumpy Gilbert Harding, who demanded perfection!

inserted a type of surgical instrument, before suddenly raising the invisible item to his mouth! Cora Portillo still remembers actually watching Henry's performance: "Henry made a comical gesture with his hand before raising it towards his mouth, it was all rather perplexing."

Needless to say, no matter how the four panellists probed and queried, Henry stood his ground and subsequently 'Beat the Panel', thereby gaining a well-earned parchment diploma. As a result he had enrolled as a new member of a small yet elite band of successful contestants – a fascinating group, somewhat bizarrely led by one of the game's funniest competitors, a sagger maker's bottom-knocker![9]

A more detailed and formal account of Henry's somewhat zany victory over the panellists was recorded by the journalist Philip Phillips of the *Daily Express*:

The Peach Taster

Earlier the Princess had gone into the TV Theatre – the Old Shepherds Bush Empire – to see "What's My Line?" She sat between Sir Ian Jacob, Director General of the BBC, and Sir George Barnes, head of TV, in the circle. Chairman Eamonn Andrews introduced the programme and the panel – Lady Barnett, Zoë Gail, Ben Lyon and Gilbert Harding – bowed to the Princess. She was intrigued with one of the competitors, Mr. Henry Stirling, from Stanmore, Middlesex, who is a "peach taster". She laughed and clapped at his mime which he later explained portrayed him taking the temperature of peaches.

The Lost Cat

A whining background noise was puzzling the theatre audience. Mr Robert McCall, a TV chief who was with the Princess' party, went to investigate. He found a black cat mewing in a corridor and chased it away. The Princess' visit lasted about three hours. Before she left she was guest of honour at a champagne party in studio H. Artists who appeared on TV last night were there. They included the "What's My Line?" panel and Harry Green, David Attenborough and Billy Cotton.

One can easily imagine the tremendous fun Henry had at the end-of-show champagne party, not least with the outspoken broadcaster and veteran panellist Gilbert Harding, once described as being the rudest man in Britain. Many will remember how the grumpy and sharp-tongued Harding, despite being an intellectual of some merit, would bully and intimidate guests if they gave evasive answers or if they spoke English less perfectly than he did. Undeniably, poor pronunciation and mumbled diction were matters that frequently annoyed the well-spoken and sophisticated Harding, who had taught English in Canada and upon the continent. In truth, many viewers admitted that Harding's frequent clashes with the less fluent and very Irish-sounding Eamonn Andrews, and his repetitive outpourings of rage over almost anything that happened to agitate him, were the programme's main attractions.

What banter must have occurred between Henry and Harding? What eloquently delivered wit? Even more fascinating: just who, one wonders, fared the better from the exciting encounter and the pointed parrying of two needle-sharp minds?

As usual, the healing of time has shown that there was another, more charitable, side to the Cambridge-educated linguist and ill-tempered Gilbert Charles Harding – an eminently more human side, which few people recognised or came to know; a side governed by an inner warmth, kindness and immense generosity. How very touched and impressed he must have been with the educated Henry, particularly his extremely cultured voice and articulately spoken English. Any suddenly formed admiration would have been greatly enhanced during their get-together by Henry's very kind gift of several delicious nectarines. This considerate gesture later prompted a softer more gentle Harding to write a short formal letter of thanks.[10]

C/o the B.B.C., London, W. 1.
13th February 1956

Dear Mr. Sterling [sic],
How very kind of you to give me the nectarines last Monday night. I ate them with the Cornish cream given to me by the mayor of Dartmouth and I couldn't possibly have enjoyed them more.
It was most kind of you and I'm very grateful to you.
Yours sincerely,
Gilbert Harding.

ACT III

"We are assigning the case to Detective Inspector Grove, Mr.
Temple. I'd be glad if you and Mr. Benson would tell him all
you know. . . . I reckon we've got a case, Temple, if those prints
tally. . . . A dart filled with formic acid in the Tiger's pelt . . . "
from *Paul Temple* by **Francis Durbridge**

Henry's engaging manner and irresistible spirit led him towards
all manner of bold adventures, yet the indubitable Henry had
so much more. He exuded a strange and powerful alchemy that
could even transmute the humble act of reverence offered at Mass
into a golden fellowship of networking fun. As a consequence,
Sunday worship at St Dunstan's was most certainly a very far cry
from being a staid and prescriptive weekly habit. To Henry the
gathering together of parishioners under the spiritual guidance of
Father Foley provided yet another blissful occasion where after
prayer and communion he could enjoy the company of close friends
and family, and the many others who shared his Catholic views.

On one such Sunday morning during the sixties, Henry had
occasion to speak to John Joseph McNamara, a freelance pen-and-
ink artist who several years earlier had left his native shores of
New Zealand to find fame and fortune in Fleet Street. By the time
of their meeting John had become a most respected artist and had
earned a first-class reputation. His first commission had come by
way of the editor of the *Daily Mail*, who had asked him to work on
the extremely popular *Captain Hornblower* strip.

Although John was extremely quiet and unassuming, the old
adage that opposites attract came quickly to the fore; and, in spite
of recognising that his new friend was fun-loving, boisterous and
rather unruly, these contrasting character traits were unimportant.
The discovery of Henry's craggy chin and his excellent bone
structure were far more interesting, and as John glanced towards
the distinguished Henry, he instinctively knew that he was looking
at the weathered face of the dogged Detective Inspector Grove.

As an influential member of Fleet Street society, the astute John
McNamara was confident that Henry's rather aristocratic profile
would be ideal as a model for the intrepid detective who frequently
and so painstakingly worked alongside the celebrated sleuth, Paul
Temple – the creation of the veteran playwright and author Francis

Durbridge.

Despite having an eye for detail, it was most unlikely that John ever contemplated that this particular serialisation, originally written for BBC radio and television, would captivate and entertain the public at large for six years. Indeed, during those years, under the guise of the straight-talking detective inspector, Henry's portrait appeared regularly within the pages of the *Evening News*.[11] Another fascinating feature that John considered worthy of note was Henry's imaginative dress sense – particularly his passion for wearing bow ties, even whilst at work. Although deemed a little too dressy for the Inspector, John recognised the impact that could be generated by a smartly dressed Paul Temple, who was usually called upon for help at very short notice, and invariably whilst dining or at the theatre. As a consequence John, with Henry's bow ties in mind, would often portray the dashing Paul Temple suitably attired.

Mary McNamara, John's widow, can still remember the actual day that Henry called at their home in Woking in order to allow her husband to take preliminary sketches:

'We had met Henry and Betty very much earlier at Church and had become quite friendly, but it was without question Henry's sturdy features that I suspect caused John to probably visualise Henry as being the ideal candidate for portraying either a gallant Police Officer or a noble high ranking officer in the military. In any event it was one morning after John had completed his daily three quarters of an hour constitutional that Henry called. They both retired to John's studio at the bottom of the garden, and then and as if by magic Henry had been transformed into Inspector Grove. I'm sure that you will understand that I am so terribly biased, but John's work was simply wonderful and Henry's face was so immensely strong. Together they formed a perfect match, and one that proved to be so highly successful.

'On the social side it was always such a shame that John was naturally quiet and rather shy because we both really enjoyed Henry and Betty's company and of course their splendid parties. Alas however the occasions were usually far too much for John who preferred smaller and more intimate gatherings.'

Detective Inspector Grove – Henry's twin.

Three examples of the old newspaper cuttings that were found hidden away in Betty's bureau.

CHAPTER SEVEN

Parties, Fishing and Bonfires

ACT I

*'I remember such happy times at Park Road as children, on those
many after school visits. I also remember Henry making fishing
flies, the only time I have ever seen it done. Of course there were
your famous New Year parties with Henry's voice heard above
all others. Henry had such a sense of fun – do you remember him
making a speech at our wedding and how he listed and compared
all the names that Cas could possibly stand for?'*
Lu, Cas, Sara and Dominic, Allestree, Derby

Just why Henry decided to leave the Stanmore district of North
West London and venture towards the county of Surrey, and the
busy railway town of Woking, remains yet another uncertainty.
Logically, however, with its excellent main-line rail service to
Waterloo, and subsequently the City, or to Victoria via a change at
the huge terminal at Clapham Junction, the town was ideally situated
for Henry and many thousands of London-bound commuters. There
is, however, one certainty that cannot in any way be challenged:
Henry's unconditional love of Moor Cottage in Woking's Park Road.
To Henry, the reasonably large and somewhat old-fashioned brick
and tile-hung dwelling could easily have embellished a pretty village
deep within the quaintness of the West Country rather than adorn a
residential link road connecting lower Maybury to the town centre
and its railway station. It was simply the one and only house of his
dreams. With spacious accommodation that included a nursery and
playroom as well as a scullery, the magnificent five-bedroom

country cottage with its secluded and mature gardens set in a good half-acre was also so reminiscent of his childhood home in Kashmir. Not only was it eminently more lavish than the Stanmore semi in Bush Grove, but the cottage also embodied the kind of family home Henry wanted for his children. It had excellent shopping and schooling facilities, and its location was within a few minutes' walk of open common land. In every way the house was perfect.

After having received notice of the customary structural survey report, which was successfully completed on the property in November 1958, a new burst of activity entered Henry's hectic life. His next move most certainly required haste. To ensure that his young family could enjoy the forthcoming holidays it had been essential to complete the move from Stanmore before that coming Christmas. Moreover, he needed to join the congregation at St Dunstan's, the local Catholic church, in order that he could give thanks and praise for his unquestionably good fortune, especially as the favourable report included a highly relevant finding:

Planning

The property faces almost due North which will mean that the rear of the house will receive the sun practically the entire day.
    Moldram, Clarke & Edgley, Chartered Surveyors & Auctioneers.[1]

All the while Henry together with his friend Tony Salamon, a partner in a North Finchley firm of solicitors, was finalising the conveyancing and financial arrangements, Betty was busy attending to the needs and demands of the three children. Whereas Jennifer (aged twelve) and David (aged ten) were by now very capable youngsters, well able to fend for themselves, Fiona, the fun-loving two-year-old affectionately called Fifi, who had become the apple of Henry's eye, was still very much a handful. With a huge new home and garden to explore and to get lost within (although Moor Cottage would lend itself perfectly for games of hide-and-seek in the future), for the time being at least, the adventurous Fifi required constant attention and supervision.

One can understand and sympathise with Betty, for although as the crow flies the distance from Woking to Stanmore is possibly less than twenty-five miles, in reality the practical problems of keeping in touch with her previous friends and neighbours, with whom she had religiously shared afternoons drinking numerous cups of tea, were almost insurmountable. Another reality of that period was that for the vast majority of stay-at-home mothers and housewives, public buses and trains were very often the only means of transport available, making Betty more or less confined to her new home or reliant upon a short bus ride into Woking town centre.

With limited help from Henry, who, after an extremely brisk fifteen-minute walk to the railway station, was commuting daily by train into Waterloo, and who was usually busy either fishing or working on the house or in the garden most weekends, Betty began networking for companionship. In the face of such opposition from Henry's amazing decision to recuperate in India and the need to simply get on with things, quiet confidence and steely boldness had long been features of Betty's renewed character. Needless to say, with Betty's interesting past and of course the antics of her highly controversial husband, friends were quickly made. Soon after, the sound of children laughing and enjoying themselves could frequently be heard in the enchanting rear garden of her spacious new home. The old and tested saying that proclaims 'In order to have friends, be one!' had once again proved to be sound and worthwhile advice. Moreover, if the truth were known, Betty was probably one of many scores of women locally who were in very similar domestic arrangements; it was just that Betty, with the indomitable Henry to cope with, had quickly learnt the art of self-preservation!

Whatever one's political persuasion, having a need for companionship where a common goal can possibly help cement even closer ties, there was much that could be said in favour of the Conservative Party in the late fifties. Indeed, to an audience at Bedford in 1957, the mature and gentlemanly Prime Minister Harold Macmillan (his first Christian name of Maurice was always discarded) uttered these immortal words:

'Let us be frank about it – most of our people have never had it so good. Go around the country, go to the industrial towns, go to the farms, and you will see a state of prosperity such as we have never had in my lifetime – nor indeed in the history of this country.'[2]

While all this Churchillian-style rhetoric may well have been true, as soon as the economy had recovered from a slight downturn, Super Mac or Mac-Wonder, as he was dubbed, decided it would be prudent to go to the country on a vote of confidence. Quite amazingly, in the October of 1959, the electorate had listened to the wise old man of politics and as a consequence had returned the Conservative Party into power. With their associates in Northern Ireland, the Tories had now twenty-one additional members able to vote in the Lower House. With the eminently more astute Tories winning three consecutive general elections, something without precedent in British political history, for better or for worse Macmillan and his electorate appeared very much at ease with one another, making a strong and sound vantage point from which Henry could successfully apply for Conservative Party membership.

During the next few years or so, as far as politics was concerned, however, Henry quickly became thoroughly disillusioned. In spite of the Tory Party growing from strength to strength in the political landscape of the South-East, and although by joining his local Conservative Association he had established a good circle of fishing companions and like-minded friends, nationally, much to the dismay of Henry, Macmillan and his government were beginning to fall into complete disarray. Macmillan's very first dilemma was Africa, where the Commonwealth was under considerable strain. Next came Europe and the extremely arrogant antics of the French president, the churlish Charles de Gaulle, who on 21 December 1958 had become leader of the Fifth Republic. The mischievous de Gaulle appeared to take great delight in upsetting everyone; in Africa he immediately incurred the enmity of colonists as well as a group of powerful army officers – both civilians and soldiers having originally expected him to back their concept of *'Algerie Francaise'*. On a similar theme he ventured to North America where he deliberately antagonised the Canadian Government with inflammatory rhetoric proclaiming *"Quebecois Liberté!"* Although this abrasive manner was calculated, his overall foreign policy was particularly straightforward: to restore and maintain the past greatness of France and achieve for her a position as leader of Europe, poised between the superpowers of the United States and the Soviet Union. With these aims accomplished, grandeur and status would follow, especially if he could flatter West Germany into a secondary role. There was of course one major obstacle to de Gaulle's whimsical fantasy: those awkward British that wished to join their European colleagues in a free-trade agreement. Determined that Britain would not wreck his chances of becoming the homespun President of Europe, de Gaulle gleefully uttered the first of several noes to the United Kingdom's request to join the

European Common Market.

At home the frustrated Macmillan fared little better. Successive budgets targeted private spending, and unemployment surged towards a million. Almost everything was going wrong. So great was the mess that the tired and increasingly frail Macmillan carried out a purge, the scale of which would have made the ruthless Stalin appear compassionate. At a political stroke he unceremoniously dismissed six cabinet ministers.

Unlike an occasion that was to follow several years later, Henry, in spite of being thoroughly disappointed, was surprisingly sympathetic to the government's plight and about its overall poor performance. Like so many others within the party, especially with his past experiences of troubled India, he too could recognise that the world was changing at such a rapid pace that, both home and abroad, political misjudgements and errors were somewhat inevitable. Happy in the knowledge that, at least for his young family, all appeared to be venturing well, he continued with his tried and tested approach to life – the carefree and cheery style of *carpe diem*.

Bearing in mind Henry's philosophy of living for today, even those who by their very nature are shy and somewhat introverted enjoy spending some quality time with close friends and family; and nothing could be more customary or pleasurable than sharing a drink and gossiping over more or less trivia whilst relaxing for a few hours in a warm comfortable room and enjoying good food. In fact, no party can ever be seen as complete without some delicacy to nibble on.

Having made this point, however, there are those who would argue that these social gatherings, although extremely congenial affairs, are not parties in the true sense of the word; to them a get-together or an old-fashioned knees-up needs a vast array of festive or popular music to get people in the mood for fun. Regrettably, if Henry had one major weakness in life, it was his failure to embrace with any enthusiasm a taste for melody. Apart from cheerily singing along to the selection of songs played by the Reigate-born Jean Metcalf, who presented the hugely popular radio show *Two Way Family Favourites* during the regular Sunday lunchtime drives in the Surrey and Sussex countryside, and thereafter entertaining Betty and the children with his own very comical rendition of 'Old Man River', to Henry, music and song remained an obscurity. Whereas there is little doubt that he fully understood the science of sound, the flow of alternating compressions and rarefactions in the air, and other obscure facts including the speed at which sound travels (about 335 metres per second), he had no interest in any musical harmony and even the ethereal quality of the singing of a choir in a lofty cathedral would have been wasted on him. Undeniably, while Beethoven's unabridged Seventh Symphony would have been much too tedious to endure, Mozart's work, especially *The Marriage of Figaro*, would have been far too deafening. And in 1962, in keeping with Decca Recording Company and several others in the business, including HMV, Henry would have refused to cross the River Mersey to sign the Liverpudlian Beatles. More to the point, however, Henry's indifference to cultured classical music would have certainly extended to pop, rap and party numbers, making the playing of 'Dancing Queen' by Abba or the singing along to the monotonous lyrics of 'Hi-Ho Silver Lining' by Jeff Beck at one of his parties not only totally superfluous, but particularly tiresome. Parties such as that were not for the loquacious Henry.

Should any deviation from the norm be called for, however – particularly a fancy-dress party – Henry would never shy away from the challenge. His most popular attire would usually include the magnificent top hat and tails, the obligatory bow tie and the elegant walking cane so readily associated with the impecunious Mr Wilkins Micawber, the extremely jaunty and carefree Dickensian character.

The impecunious Mr Wilkins Micawber.

Many who have read the tale of *David Copperfield* will remember the imprudent spendthrift from a time when David worked at Murdstone and Grinby's warehouse and needed somewhere nearby to lodge. Although very much like the equally optimistic and good-natured Henry, the rather improvident Mr Micawber, who, incidentally, also shared a passion for living for today, yet beyond his means, makes no provision for the future, always hoping that something would turn up to extricate him from his difficulties.

Such were the scenes upon which Henry Stirling and his zany laugh became known – social gatherings of good fellowship, good food and good wine. These were occasions where light-hearted fun was the order of the day and where the skilful Henry shone.

'In the happy and relaxed atmosphere of your home, Henry was such fun with a host of amusing anecdotes and stories, which Andrew still repeats to all our friends.'

Jen and Andrew, Newmarket, Suffolk

'Henry was such a lovely, jolly man (we will always remember his infectious laugh) and we have very fond memories of him.'

Duncan and Penny Jack

'We will all miss Henry's humour at parties and other places we used to meet. He always cheered me up.'

Eve, Woking, Surrey

'Henry was a dear man with wonderful humour. He was always fun to meet and talk to and could be relied upon to enliven any gathering.'

Pat, Woking, Surrey

'I loved Henry's impish twinkle in his eyes when he was saying something to try and shock you or pull you up with a start at some outrageous statement. But he was only teasing, and that banal face and smile always belied whatever his tongue might have said. Oh, we shall miss him.'

Gloria H.

'Henry was such a lovely man – so full of fun and somehow made one feel happier for meeting him. No party was complete without Henry! He really will be missed by everyone.'

Marion, Woking, Surrey

The party-loving Henry, having decided that his particular chosen course in life would always include fun and laughter, made little attempt to conceal it from others. As a consequence, everyone fortunate to have known him soon realised that he had been blessed with a hugely disproportionate sense of humour. This was especially so of his closer friends, who all knew that Henry was more than capable of inciting mayhem, laughter and annoyance in the most unlikely of settings. Indeed, Peter Paine, who was both a fishing companion and close friend, paints a splendid picture of their badly behaved yet wonderful friendship. With great charm and unwavering loyalty Peter took immense delight in recollecting how Henry's impish behaviour was certainly never prescriptive to any given time or to any particular place:

'I can recall an occasion when Henry had hoodwinked me into helping out at the Conservative Summer Fair. It was their annual fund raising event, which was held by kind permission of the Terrys at their enormous home and garden within the private and prodigious grounds of the Hockering. It must be understood that this occurred way back and these grand garden events were all rather formal affairs. The Terrys were very well known in Conservative circles; James who ended the war as a major was a former chairman of Woking Council. I am also pretty sure that, at the time, he was actually the president of the Maybury and Mount Hermon Conservative Branch where Elizabeth was also the lady Club president.
    'Henry, completely oblivious to pointed groans of despair from several committee members who were always against the suggestion, decided to install and run a coconut shy, and as I have said, he also volunteered my services. Much to the annoyance and utter frustration of the Terrys our makeshift coconut stall brought as much chaos to the event as it did success. A few members, those who Henry always referred to as the Old Tory Guard, were really appalled by his raucous behaviour, whilst several others appeared to be deeply offended almost outraged by Henry's own unique recitation of "I've got a lovely bunch of coconuts – big ones, small ones and some as big as your wife, the idol of me life" and his repetitive cries of "Roll a bowl a ball, roll a bowl a ball, singing roll a bowl a ball a penny a pitch." Henry's booming laugh and persistent chuckling could easily be heard above all others, and became especially so after he had decided to ensure that no one could actually win a prize. He cunningly ensnarled the coconuts so

firmly that not even a direct hit could dislodge them from their stands. Though in fairness to Henry, if a child or one of his closer friends participated he would very willingly hand over a well-earned reward. Needless to say as a direct result of Henry's enthusiasm, particularly the din that had arisen around his shy, we were both very unpopular with more than just a few fervent dissenters, and this was in spite of our fund raising achievement. Apparently some Conservative members had been so very distressed by the whole episode that for many years thereafter the fair was known locally as "the fête worse than death". Looking back however, although the Terrys thought that Henry had lowered the tone somewhat, nothing could have been further from the truth – it was just good wholesome fun with Henry, as usual, at the helm.'

In 1973 these jocular episodes of *Fun, Flies and Laughter* were abruptly brought to a very dramatic end. Henry was to experience his first serious heart attack. Yet, after a brief period of tentative convalescing, and without *any* fuss or unnecessary commotion, it was work as usual. And by all accounts it seems that there was little change in Henry's demeanour. Laughter beamed from his office so his work-friends and colleagues knew all was well.

Looking back over the aftermath of Henry's second encounter with dire ill fortune, however, his extremely devoted secretary recalls how his welcome return to duty only provided a short-lived period of joy and optimism:

'When Henry suffered his first heart attack Sandy and I decorated one wall of his office with balloons, streamers and "welcome back" banners – he didn't see them until he sat at his desk and looked up. I think he was suitably pleased; although his return to work turned out to be a little premature and we had to have another "welcome back" a few months later.'

Sadly, throughout the seventies far more dangerous attacks were to follow, and such was their increasing magnitude that Henry required urgent bypass surgery. The long-drawn-out act of recovery, however, brought down the curtain on Henry's managerial career at the Deciduous Fruit Board. In spite of an extremely successful operation he was advised on grounds of ill health to seek an early retirement. Weaker than ever before, and acutely debilitated from years of constant uncertainty, the cardiac specialist considered that he would require several years of quality time to fully recover. There was, however, one blessing: in the period of convalescence, and despite an absolute ban on strenuous activity where brawn as well as brain was required, the crafty rather teasing struggle of fly-fishing was to be allowed. It appears that everyone, including his medical advisers, knew of Henry's canny and vast experience of the sport and were equally aware that he could land a fish with guile and cunning, discarding any need for arduous exertion.

Once again it seemed that Henry's privileged yet uncertain life was to turn a page. Moreover, nothing was more natural for him than to press forward by paradoxically making a retreat to a lifestyle that had served him well throughout: a life of *Fun, Flies and Laughter*!

What a wonderful job – fruit, fun and laughter!

Henry with the dutiful and smiling Betty.

ACT II

THE FISHERMAN

He fishes in the morning, he fishes late at night;
He fishes in foul weather, and when the sun is bright,
He fishes, fishes, fishes, it's his only thing in life,
And all he ever catches is HELL from his fed-up wife.

Henry, always the optimist, took the shock and initial disruption of retirement with pragmatic composure. By the summer of 1977 he had managed to overcome and adapt to the many uncertainties of his bizarre life, and had learnt to accept its rich and complicated pageant. More than this, through personal experiences of combat, he fully understood the utter futility of attempting to outmanoeuvre the invisible and the impractical folly of second-guessing what was so obviously unpredictable. Running parallel with these extremely sensible qualities was his reputation as quite a character, a kind and endearing maverick that was usually the very heart and soul of any social gathering. Somewhat inevitably, therefore, Henry's colourful personality tended to set him apart from others around him, although, as previously cited, it would be wrong to suggest that he deliberately associated himself with run-of-the-mill mediocrity. On the contrary, Henry's interpersonal skills were formidable – a quality that enabled him to converse with absolutely anyone who just so happened to cross his path. Furthermore, to Henry stature and esteem were not prerequisites for interesting debate. Indeed, it was because of this rather unassuming quality that, in keeping with other vibrant personalities of this wonderful era, Henry's deeds and foibles were very seldom seen in any true sense of proportion. In most cases, both his fun-loving adventures and his boisterous habits attracted either extravagant praise or ardent condemnation. It is, though, generally accepted by all those who knew him that the fun-loving Henry was a truly exceptional game fisherman with a vast and excellent knowledge of the sport – particularly the making of flies.

With these fine words of appraisal in mind, quite what Henry would have made of the best-selling *Encyclopaedia of an Ordinary Life* by Amy Krouse Rosenthal, in which the author claims that life's best thrills come not from sport, super-de luxe cruises or haute couture but from having a friend bake you a pie, is perhaps best left unsaid; for Henry simply adored his fishing and nothing could surpass its pleasures. On reflection, whether like Henry you are a considered expert or an enthusiastic amateur, it is easy to understand the appeal of fly-fishing: standing on a remote riverbank, rod in hand, surrounded by water, lush forest or woodland, and occasional blue sky. After all, the sport not only encourages anglers to get away from the crowds, but many would have agreed with Henry the botanist that communing with nature is just as important to the pursuit as flies, lines and reeling in a big catch.

However pertinent these factors may first appear, and in spite of Henry's immense skill and passion for the sport, it seems that Henry's sense of fun and old-fashioned slapstick were less endearing features that would on occasions very inconveniently dovetail. Once again there could not be a better upstanding witness than Peter Stanley Paine, DFC (CBE, 1981). Like Henry, Flight Lieutenant Paine had also experienced several torrid times during the course of the Second World War. His first daring task had been to fly the underpowered Bristol Blenheim Mk I, a three-seat light bomber that had started life as a high-speed light transport plane. Operationally, however, the difficult-to-handle aircraft quickly acquired a notorious reputation as a poor performer and of being particularly vulnerable.[3] As a consequence, having survived more

Three happy men – one Midas touch.

than his fair share of hair-raising sorties and recognising the folly of believing that he was invincible, adopting a spirit similar to Henry's seemed a most sensible way forward; from then on he too would live for today. Unlike the indomitable Henry, however, Peter, who eventually became managing director of Tyne-Tees Television, encountered many more practical difficulties than his fishing companion. As a result, many precious years had passed before he could finally begin to practise Henry's carefree philosophy. In the early eighties, after having been advised by a close friend and editor at ITN, Sir Geoffrey Cox, to take up fly-fishing, and after having returned from Northumberland to his home in Surrey, Peter quickly re-established his associations in Woking and forged an even closer bond with the redoubtable and like-minded Henry. At first their liaison and Peter's renewed vision upon life brought them to fish on lakes at Clandon, owned by Lord Onslow, and thereafter upon Mallards Mere, Herons Reach and Pikes Pool, the three major lakes at Effingham, on land still owned and managed by Peter Skinner.

Henry's stalwart fishing partner and extremely good friend can still recall one particular visit to Effingham where Henry's rebellious behaviour played a major role in the day's proceedings:

'On one occasion I had invited my friend Graham Mack to join us at Effingham, where it is well known that it is far better to secure a

boat and fish out water rather than find a beat along the banks. So after having spotted others approaching Mallards Mere all three of us scampered after the two boats that were moored nearby. Henry always fleet of foot immediately took possession of the nearest boat and then much to my surprise invited Graham to accompany him, rather tersely leaving me on my own. That though was not the problem, that came a little later, when to Henry's immense delight, and whilst he was cheerfully drinking whisky they began to enjoy great success, making my endeavours appear rather feeble. Then, and as if to add insult to injury, the incorrigible rogues who thought the whole affair was simply hilarious did nothing to reconcile my plight – they merrily continued quaffing to their success without even bothering to pass me the bottle!

'Joking aside however Henry was a really talented game fisherman, and on one occasion in Ireland, fishing the River Moy, his true knowledge and understanding of the sport became abundantly clear. Henry's keen eye and vast awareness of the different species of flies enabled us to replace our pseudo replicas and select the fly that our prey had been taking so vigorously. As a result we all benefited and achieved tremendous success. Yet with most larger than life characters especially the Henrys of this world, there was of course another side to his temperament, a mischievous side that could often cause laughter yet at the very same time great annoyance. I distinctly remember another occasion in Ireland when I had managed to secure the best beat along the estuary. It wasn't too long before I had a salmon on the line and was beginning to play it. All the time I remember having this firm belief that even more success was coming my way when suddenly Betty bellowed at me. Her actual words will always send a shiver down my spine, "Peter, I am really angry with Henry." What happened next was understandable yet perhaps unforgivable. Naturally the commotion not only caused a lack of concentration on my part but in one split second the salmon had taken full advantage of the situation and had escaped. Bemused and equally angry as the distressed Betty I immediately retorted, "Bugger off Betty." However with the whole episode quickly becoming a French farce, I did the gentlemanly thing by apologising and asking her what had happened. The very next moment a dishevelled Henry had appeared looking like a drowned rat. Once again his enthusiasm had got the better of him, and he *had become over excited and so typical of Henry he had fallen into the water. The comical situation takes on a graver significance after Betty had explained that the fishing trip was taken against medical advice and that as a result of his careless plunge he had lost all of his medication. Still fuming over the loss of my salmon, I have to admit that my initial reaction was one of sheer indifference, and I responded as if completely untroubled by Henry's foolishness.'*

Against a background of fun, foolishness and joviality, however, when it came to knowing your flies, Henry was an expert. Having made flies from his early childhood and having studied the subject as though his very soul depended on their every whim and lifelike daintiness, he could simply not be equalled – a skill and attribute often reflected upon by others:

'I remember the long chats with Henry about flies and the fishing at Effingham. I shall certainly miss our conversations. He knew so much about the natural insects and I learnt a lot from him. We last met in the September where he had been fishing and I was just starting. I shall miss his cheery "hello" at the lakes.'
John Sawfell, Woking, Surrey

'Yes I should love two or three small salmon flies as a reminder of Henry. I think they should all be the same as I could risk using one or two (I mean of course risk losing one or two for I am not the expert Henry was).'
Dr Michael Raymond, Worth, Sussex

Any study of Henry's fishing career would illustrate how a boyish romanticism of his early life in India, and the extremely fortunate and nostalgic period that he spent in convalescence, undeniably meant that Henry would have always preferred fishing the magnificent lakes of Kashmir to anywhere else. From all accounts, however, it seems that the extremely picturesque River Esk in Scotland, and the lakes and rivers that straddle Counties Mayo and Sligo in Ireland came very close. Accordingly, Henry, who in spite of enjoying the true splendour of bonnie Scotland and in particular the fruitful waters that are formed by the joining of the rivers North and South Esk, considered above all others the calm sanctuary of North-West Ireland a fisherman's haven. Without any reservation he would have agreed upon these outstanding descriptions:

'The Moy has long been Ireland's most prodigious salmon river and offers a wide variety of quality angling. Most of the main Moy channel, and some of its larger tributaries provide excellent spring salmon and grilse fishing with flies and bait. Sea trout are also abundant in the Moy and the dry fishing brown trout can also be excellent.'[4]

Making flies somewhere in Ireland.

The main Moy channel is idyllically deep and wide, and as a result vast numbers of salmon are landed each season.

'The rich lowland limestone rivers and loughs are home to heavy, fast-growing trout which are selective feeders and make challenging sport.'[5]

'The Erriff System is comprised of the Erriff River and the loughs of Tawnyard and Derrintin. The River Erriff is a premier salmon fishing river in Ireland, characterised by lively streams and deep fish-holding miles of prime angling water, divided into 9 beats.'[6]

Fortuitously, Henry's fishing diaries reveal the enormous pleasure he derived from his visits to both Scotland and Western Ireland, and, although there are simply far too many instances to illustrate, the following more prominent entries help capture Henry's passion, skill and enjoyment from not only the demanding sport but the delight he held for both inherited homelands.

River Esk

29.8.55
Started fishing shortly after 8 p.m. in shallow pool below Byne Barn Foot [?]. Moved nothing till it was dark at about 9. By 9.30 the fish were taking really well. Fished until 12. The night was fine and the moon shone occasionally. No other rods [fishermen] were fishing in the vicinity. Killed 1 sea trout.

30.8.55
Again nothing until it was dark. The night was fine and the moon was full. Killed a sea trout. Many other fishermen arrived subsequently, but killed few fish. They were all using worm.

Erriff

29.7.86
There had been heavy rain the previous day but the river was dropping. Started on beat 6 and hooked a sea trout and rose another. Moved down and got a sea trout at the south tail of a large pool. After lunch went to beat 5 and started halfway up a long run. Soon killed sea trout and then another.

30.7.86
Beat 3. Moved to long run below heavily tried stretch near road. Towards the bottom of this run hooked a salmon and after a protracted fight landed it. Resumed fishing and a little further up killed two large sea trout and hooked another. Then hooked a salmon, which played for about 20 minutes and threw the hook.
    After lunch went downstream and fished school (home or house) reach

where a second salmon was hooked. After a long fight it was netted.

No more fish were caught but at around 6 Geoffrey [Dr Ambrose] hooked a sea trout on the top pool of the beat.

Both salmon and smallest sea trout caught on shrimp fly. Larger sea trout on C..en..an[?]. Black. All fish were hooked on rise while backing up.

Tawnyard

31.7.86
Fished all day with G. A. [Dr Ambrose] Many small brown caught, but no sea trout risen although some were jumping at the top end of the lake.

At the same time as enjoying success, however, Henry was not immune or shielded from days when, no matter how he endeavoured, fish would not rise to the bait. Indeed, the final diary illustration reveals that not even a generous River Moy could always guarantee a day of glorious achievement.

River Moy

26.6.91
Ash Tree Beat. The day was calm and the river at a moderate height. Spent most of the day fishing from boat. Salmon were showing in numbers from time to time, but although occasional fish may have looked at the flies, none took. Also tried spinning.

ACT III

'Observations have shown that a single fire greatly reduces disease for the first season and often to a lesser extent for the second. This reduction in disease permits foliage retention through the second season, a condition necessary for optimum seedling development.'

P. V. Siggers, 1932, *Forest Pathology* by J. S. Boyce, MA, MF, PhD

During the early eighties, although political correctness was in its infancy the environmentalist lobby throughout Europe had gained immense popularity. The Green Party had secured their first members of the European Parliament and Greenpeace protesters had achieved tremendous notoriety by successfully performing some truly spectacular stunts. Henry Stirling, however, was not one easily swayed by gimmicks and unsubstantiated ideals, and, to coin a phrase, he believed in evolution not revolution. This assessment, however, is not a criticism of the knowledgeable Henry, but a measure of his true understanding of the environment in which we live. His degree in botanical forestry had left him exceptionally well informed upon a wide array of ecological dilemmas, ranging from the very grave concerns over greenhouse gases and the ozone layer to the more basic principles of forest pathology including mystifying stem diseases with names like galls and witches' broom! With such a vast awareness at his disposal, Henry was a formidable opponent of the forever-increasing anti-burning cult. What was more telling was that apart from the very occasional and genuinely held grievance by a neighbour complaining that their washing was being exposed to woodsmoke, it became a pointless exercise for anyone with only a limited grasp of the subject to try to restrict his passion for burning contaminated garden waste including the roots of bindweed and couch grass and evergreen leaves such as holly. The open-minded Henry, who was perfectly in tune with how modern living was rapidly and dangerously increasing carbon monoxide, was more than able to counter and refute any claim of recklessness made by those who would carelessly introduce ill-informed judgement upon the environment or utter totally spurious arguments. With greater knowledge and understanding as the key, Henry displayed an air of confidence in the future of our ever-changing world. He stood firm in the belief that the growth of environmental anarchy (one cause of the earth's surface being warmed by solar radiation) would not be curtailed by way of liberalism, godliness or passion, but by quarrelsome industrialists, brilliant scientists and dedicated engineers. Moreover, it would be this curious amalgam of talent that would arrange a way round the problem, and not the linking of hands by naked cranks chanting peace programmes or by the making of insincere pledges of goodwill.

Taking up this issue further and returning to Henry's wonderful garden, as an extremely talented and keen gardener he adored the autumn, particularly as daylight began to fade and when a warming drink was being prepared as a reward for his afternoon's labour. For Henry, autumn was not a time for despair or troublesome concerns over the days becoming shorter; it was a time for carefully prepared bonfires and potash, and it was a period when he would invite neighbours to deposit their carefully gathered leaves upon one of his numerous heaps of compost and leaf mould. To Henry, ever conscious of nature's blessings, these bundles of colourful foliage that had earlier adorned our gardens with red, yellow and golden splendour, were not annoying leaves past their best but a valuable source of nutrients only needing fungal activity to produce dark brown crumbly garden mulch. Against a backdrop of growing political correctness Henry stood resolute, particularly over the true value of potash – an inexpensive fertiliser and a splendid source of carbonate of potassium. He instinctively knew that, in general, old wood contained more potash than younger growth and that best results came from slow burning. On a more practical point he also knew how his prized fruit garden, especially the currant and gooseberry bushes, enjoyed devouring the burnt residue, and how dry wood ash helps to neutralise the acidity in soil, known technically as achieving the correct pH level. Without doubt those initial few weeks of autumn bliss – a period of fun and bonfires – brought Henry as much pleasure as it did toil, especially if he could experience the joy of harvesting maincrop potatoes – late varieties that reach maturity as late as the beginning of November. They had very often been purposely grown by Henry, within the deep rich heaps of well-rotted garden waste.

With the certainty of cruel weather ahead, nothing came more naturally to Henry than to prepare for the following spring by commencing the lengthy but worthwhile process of putting a garden to bed for winter. Yet not everyone agreed with Henry's views, especially on the environmental benefits of burning ailing or diseased brushwood. On the contrary, a few rather self-righteous neighbours were utterly mortified at the very thought of a garden having within its compounds both a smelly compost heap and waste ground to accommodate bonfires. However, unless their complaint had some justification, a factor that hardly ever arose, Henry was not a man to confront over either a lack of consideration or upon environmental recklessness. Any woolly-minded complainants would get very short change, especially those who had either driven no more than fifty yards to air their grievance or parted with their opinions by way of moaning over the telephone.

Undaunted by the views of the PC brigade, Henry persevered with his autumn bonfires and fully utilised another aspect of their misunderstood role. Safe in the knowledge that the potassium would help raise alkalinity and encourage the welcome almost essential presence of red brandling worms, he would generously sprinkle any remaining ashes over his numerous compost heaps.

Henry, who had enjoyed a wonderful introduction to practical gardening and its various techniques by studying the principles of the well-known horticulturist, Arthur G. L. Hellyer, MBE, VMH, editor of *Amateur Gardening* and attentively listening to Professor Alan Gemmell of Keele, OBE, the long-serving panellist of the hardy Radio 4 perennial *Gardeners' Question Time*, considered such disagreeable and pedantic people as being mostly narrow-minded television gardeners obsessed by modern shredding machines. They were also ruining their homes by erecting appallingly constructed prefabricated outside extensions! On numerous occasions, especially during those gloriously warm summer afternoons, whilst idly relaxing by the entrance to his sunken rose garden sipping Earl Grey (taken with very little milk in order not to spoil the flavouring of the distinctly scented oil of bergamot), the tea-drinking and sun-worshipping Henry often spoke of these witless people. As far as he was concerned, these highly gullible souls were being fooled into creating outdoor areas from inappropriate material, which were more often than not completely out of harmony with the traditional character of their neighbourhood. To Henry, a garden traditionalist, these were the true environmental vandals – verandas were for Indian dwellings, patios were for the continentals, and the newly arrived phenomenon, North American-style decking, was just vulgar! Rural Britain should contain homes enhanced by York Stone English terraces, possibly with sundials, although well-sited Victorian conservatories were also perfectly acceptable. Indeed, such was Henry's feeling for tasteful garden architecture that it is just possible that his generic instincts were once again playing their part, inasmuch as another family namesake, Sir James Stirling (1926–1992) was the inspiration behind the RIBA Stirling Prize, the United Kingdom's most prestigious prize awarded annually for the greatest contribution to British architecture in the past year.

Another gardening bête noire of Henry's was the increase in low-maintenance projects for front gardens. He was totally dismayed by the escalating use of multi-coloured shingle, and one can only wonder what he and Professor Gemmell would have made of the more current trend of simply concreting over lawns and beds in order to create parking yards. Coincidentally, Professor Alan Gemmell and Henry's fishing pal, Peter Paine, received their awards in the same 1981 New Year's Honours List.

Henry's love for gardening, however, was literally down to earth, an appropriate testimony to the unique relationship between the gardener and his outdoor retreat. What was also apparent was his fondness for more natural or wild flora; white and red flowers of the common *Lamium album* and *Lamium purpureum* (dead-nettles), and ferns, including the highly durable bracken, were tended as if they were prize roses as opposed to dreary, oppressive vegetation. There is not any possible way that he could be described as a hobby gardener. The pastime of growing chrysanthemums or dahlias or the fussing over hanging baskets and tubs were all deemed meaningless tasks and were dismissed as not justifying such hard labour. On the other hand, and in keeping with the tasty spoils from fly-fishing, vegetables and fruit could be consumed and enjoyed thereby creating a perfectly good reason for toil.

Rising above all else, however, was Henry's passion for trees. As a boy he had enjoyed climbing to their majestic summits, and as a scholar he had studied and valued their unconditional contribution to mankind. To all intents and purposes Henry and his oxygenic friends were as one.

'I shall always remember Henry climbing trees and cutting down brambles at the bottom of our adjoining gardens when we lived in Ivy Lane.'

Hilda, Woking, Surrey

Without any doubt, it was the splendid canopy of English oaks, birches and Scots pines proudly guarding the rhododendron curtilage of Moor Cottage that caused Henry to fall hopelessly in love with his home and its wooded garden. Yet everything good has a price – a dilemma fully appreciated by Henry, who was always acutely aware that his wooded paradise would require constant care and fostering. As a consequence, Henry was forever searching out the services of a professional tree surgeon, one that he could rely upon and a true expert in his own field. More important was finding a surgeon with sound knowledge of forestry and not some fly-by-night that was just seeking cash in hand without any care, knowledge or scruples. In short, Henry, who treated every individual tree as though it was well-loved kin, wanted someone whom he could trust emphatically. Not a lover of door-to-door sales and not one for looking into newspapers or magazines on a par with *Yellow Pages*, Henry demanded more than just a glossy advert depicting rates and skills. His trees were all so very precious and only the best care would suffice.

On one Saturday morning way back in the eighties, Henry's hot pursuit for excellence finally ended. Around eight o'clock, Jim Bilston and his much older partner, Alfie, began felling a neighbour's very old Scots pine. The rather poorly tree had seen its best years and was becoming a hazard. Henry, who had been confined to bed until his admission to hospital for further heart surgery, couldn't resist monitoring the whole process of the felling from his bedroom window. Thereafter and without hesitation he gave instructions to Betty to have both Jim and Alfie come to see him. Jim recalls the incident as if it were yesterday:

'We were just packing up when Mrs Stirling spoke to us, it was always Mrs Stirling but we always got told to call Mr Stirling, Henry. Well we went straight upstairs and met him. He was in bed looking pretty shaky but was pleased over what we had done next door, he told us that he would like his Oaks topped, the ones that run along the back of the garden. We agreed to do them and arranged to come back the following week. I remember saying to Alfie "We won't get those done mate – he'll be needing a wooden overcoat soon." Alfie did made me laugh when afterwards he said something like "Jim, one sharp frost followed by a fried snowball and he's definitely a gonna." Well Henry didn't die and we did the job. From then on we did all of Henry's tree work. It was always the same routine, coffee and biscuits in the morning made by Mrs Stirling, and drinks with Henry after we got paid and before we left for home.

'I know it sounds corny but Mrs Stirling was a real lady and Henry was an absolute gent. They would always find time for a chat and ask how we were. We used to enjoy working at Moor Cottage, especially talking to Henry about politics and hearing stories about his fishing. There was one time when we even watched him smoke trout in an old glazed pot that he had propped up against a neighbour's fence just to annoy them. He was using some oak sawdust I had given him. Old Alfie used to love drinking Henry's home-made beer even if it hadn't been fermented properly, and after one Saturday session I remember Alfie being sent straight to bed, he had collapsed as soon as he got home. Another thing was that after that first job for Henry we never had to look for work again. Henry seemed to know everyone in Woking and me and Alfie got job after job. Henry must have said we were pretty good because we never got any problems whatsoever and we never had any fuss over payment.

'My fondest memory of Henry though, was the time he introduced me to Margaret Thatcher! Again it was one Saturday morning when I had called round to cut the hedges. I had only just started when it unexpectedly began to rain. As the rain became heavier Henry came out and said that I should pack up, come inside and have a drink. I wasn't worried about not being paid because I knew Henry would square things up, but as I had already gotten wet I decided to continue. As soon as I had jobbed up, Henry greeted me with his usual grin and immediately invited me into the playroom as they used to call it. I remember saying that I had better stay outside because I was still pretty wet. Henry would not hear of it and after opening the French windows he almost dragged me in. I tell you it was quite a shock to suddenly see that blooming woman sitting opposite you holding a Union Jack in one hand and her handbag in the other. It probably sounds silly but having a full size cardboard cutout of Margaret Thatcher actually sitting in the corner looking you up and down isn't very nice. Henry who knew full well that I was never too happy about her and the Conservatives, just started that laugh of his, and said "You're not particularly keen on Maggie, Jim, are you?" Before I had chance to say anything Henry had picked her up, made out that he was dancing across the room and then sat her down on the chair next to where I was standing. He then said "Go on Jim, show your disapproval; keep her quiet and sit on her!"

'After a couple of drinks and chatting about the hedge, politics cropped up again, when I started to moan about John Major and his lot. Henry really surprised me; he completely agreed with me and said that there were so many around who were behaving appallingly and that it would be fair comment to say that collectively they were an absolute shower. He even went further and said something like "Jim, the Conservatives are rapidly becoming unelectable and will remain so for many years." Little did I realise at the time that he was to be so right. I suppose that is what I liked about Henry the most; you could have a different point of view than his but he would never criticise you for it. Another thing was that he would always ask why you thought that way without trying

Maggie T in the playroom with Charlotte, Henry's youngest granddaughter.

to belittle you.

'I really miss Henry and Mrs Stirling; Woking just isn't the same any more.'

The remarkable feature of this casual conversation was that Henry's political wisdom was to come to fruition only four years after his death. Somehow he must have sensed the changing mood and political landscape of the country and had quickly realised that dogged Conservatism with a capital C was practically doomed. Logic and a grasp of realism had also made him acutely aware that sooner rather than later a seemingly united centre-left government would become eminently more favourable than yet another tired Tory government that appeared to be in such total disarray and completely out of touch with Cool Britannia. As disharmony grew and internal wrangling came to the fore, it became so abundantly clear to all but the foolish that any foreseeable Conservative establishment would be comprised of a quarrelsome hotch-potch of right and centre-right politicians within the Redwood and Portillo camps, and the "corporatist, interventionist and federalist Michael Heseltine," who was predominately more to the left.[7] Added to this confusing mix were several pro-Europeans from both the left and right of the party that were led by the highly influential Kenneth Clarke, as well as ninety-odd members of the Euro-sceptical Fresh Start Group. As matters stood, regardless of how the bewildered and battered John Major endeavoured to maintain discipline, Henry just knew that his position was untenable and that further European integration would soon act as a catalyst for the destruction of an utterly bankrupt government. Indeed, within two short years of his funeral Henry's rather forlorn prophecy began to unfold. On 22 June 1995 an angry and thoroughly disillusioned John Major sought to put an end to the internal backbiting within his cabinet as well as media speculation over his future. In the garden at Number 10 he resigned the leadership of the Conservative Party and immediately thereafter put himself forward as a candidate.

Meanwhile, and much more disturbing, both to the vast electorate and to a frustrated Henry, were the constant allegations of political sleaze that during the early sixties had suddenly engulfed his old-fashioned 1950s 'One Nation' party to such an extent that simply nobody had faith in a single word the government was saying. There can be little doubt that, by studying the flow of media condemnation, the astute Henry knew that the harangued, disjointed and much

145

vilified Conservative Party, regardless of its past successes, was destined to be defeated and was most certainly living on borrowed time.

Perhaps Henry's perceptive antenna was beginning to detect an aura of déjà vu, and he was able to recall a time when the phrase 'political sleaze' had echoed around the House of Commons before. It is more than likely that his mind was flashing back to the bawdy antics of Mandy Rice-Davies and Christine Keeler, and that he was mentally reliving the grubby circumstances that had embroiled the Conservatives in the early sixties. In the now infamous Profumo Affair, the Right Honourable John Profumo, PC, OBE, MP, Secretary of State for War, was accused of being a highly dangerous risk to national security after having apparently slept with British yet Soviet-hired prostitutes. The wretched state of the Tory Party during these uncertain times would have been well known to Henry. By an amazing coincidence, he had befriended the journalist and author Warwick Charlton, who had an intimate knowledge of that sad political period. Although it is uncertain whether they first met at university, India or in North Africa, Warwick appears to have known Henry reasonably well. Another anomaly was that the respected Charlton, who had been a wartime intelligence officer on the staffs of Montgomery and Mountbatten, and who had been mentioned in despatches at Alamein, seems to have also known the notorious and extremely influential Dr Stephen Ward. It had been Ward that had supposedly made the introductions between Profumo and Keeler and had allowed his home in Wimpole Mews to be the venue for their sordid assignations. Another coincidence, which may shed some light on how Henry could well have known of Ward, is that the Doctor's somewhat spurious medical credentials were eventually recognised by the Royal Army Medical Corps, and as a consequence Ward was granted a commission. Apparently, a great deal of mistrust had earlier been placed upon Ward's Kirksville, USA degree, a matter that caused him to suffer from 'osteopath's syndrome', inasmuch as doctors very often considered osteopaths as only curious cranks. In spite of Ward's difficulties, however, once accepted he went on to achieve reasonable success and, in common with Henry and Warwick, he also had occasion to serve in India.

Assured of a best-seller, it was Warwick Charlton's knowledge and possibly friendship for Ward, that led *Today* magazine to commission him to write an account of the long conversations he had with Ward and many of the others within the entanglement. Consequently, after the book's publication Warwick duly dispatched a signed volume to an unsuspecting Henry. Its content not only detailed the freely given yet shameful interviews, but also vividly exposed and illustrated the passions and motives that led to Jack Profumo's letter of resignation to Harold Macmillan on 4 June 1963. In a bizarre twist of fate (and of rather more significance), the extremely poignant inscription upon the first page of the paperback titled *Stephen Ward Speaks & The Profumo Affair* reads thus:

'To Henry – let this be a lesson to you – Warwick '68.'

Unquestionably, Henry, an innocent pupil in this highly dubious and sordid affair, had studied those few words rather intently. As a result, having read how so many of the political famous are prepared to remain in denial, and more often than not go to very great lengths to avoid the telling truth, Henry appears to have once again excelled in his studies, especially benefiting from Warwick Charlton's harsh lesson on British political life.

Shortly before his last illness, rather than sitting back in denial, Henry accepted the inevitable demise of a party that appeared incapable of progressing the less redundant ideals of Thatcherism. Completely at a loss over the government's neglect of more pressing domestic policies, and their constant self-inflicted bickering over Europe, Henry could only foresee folly and political skulduggery. Consequently, a disenchanted Henry Stirling, hitherto a staunch and loyal supporter, sensing that the equally torn Labour Party would present a cunningly united front on Europe in order to gain power, somewhat reluctantly resigned from his local Conservative Association. As one would expect of Henry, he refused to hide under falsehood or nebulous excuses, such as not having the time or feeling far too unwell to make any further commitment. He simply informed the local party secretary of his reasons. In a short handwritten letter, Henry addressed the issue perfectly. He initially stated that he thought the conduct of several eminent members at Westminster had been totally unacceptable. Amongst other gossip that abounded, Henry was unquestionably referring to the sordid allegations that had earlier engulfed the one-time party chairman, Jeffrey Archer. Henry, with the Profumo Affair firmly implanted in his perceptive mind, was never convinced of the wily politician's innocence, despite the ultra-confident Archer having successfully, albeit temporarily, cleared his good name. Furthermore, as matters panned out, Henry's letter of shrouded condemnation was written and delivered only a few months prior to yet another rumour becoming an overt allegation of impropriety. The extremely popular Jonathan Aitken, after eight years of denial, was eventually found guilty of perjury, regardless of being armed with his all-powerful and glittering 'sword of truth'.

Unashamed of his Britishness, and undeterred that everyone except those from the Conservative right wing would ridicule his opinions, Henry concluded his candid explanation by adding that he had considered the party's volte-face on Europe and the subsequent signing of the Maastricht Treaty an act of political cowardice.

Without question it was the signing of the Maastricht Treaty during 1991 that sounded the death knell to Henry's membership of the Conservative Party. The call for even greater European political union that would include a European single currency as well as a common European defence policy was simply taking EEC (European Economic Community) integration much too far. With the Communist Bloc in Eastern Europe disintegrating, Germany reunified, and the civil war in the former Yugoslavia raging, Henry foresaw the tender shoots of Franco-German European dominance and a scramble for rampant nationalism, similar to the 1930s when utter chaos ensued. Moreover, whereas Henry welcomed free trade and fully appreciated the global market he predicated that Europe's political stability and relatively high standard of living would subsequently create a temporary Western European haven for economic migrants and refugees and, in his own words, "all end in tears"!

CHAPTER EIGHT

In the Footsteps of Simon

ACT I

'For he [Simon Peter] and all his companions were astonished at the catch of fish they had taken, and so were James and John, the sons of Zebedee, Simon's partners. Then Jesus said to Simon, "Don't be afraid; from now on you will catch men."'

Luke 5: 9 to 11

Henry emerges from any recitation of the events of his life as a man of exceptional self-assurance. Although originating from a wonderfully privileged background, he was more than capable of making remarkably informed, realistic and down-to-earth judgements, and thereafter demonstrating a no-nonsense resolve required for keeping true to his word. What's more, even though he had been born into a family that on his father's side had for centuries held an aristocratic and pugnacious tradition, as a fun-loving fisherman Henry did not particularly welcome these ancestral attributes – past heroic exploits that so very often place a great burden upon their blameless and unsuspecting inheritors. Furthermore, whereas there may be a suggestion that Henry's acute stubbornness had been directly inherited from an eccentric mother, and that this at-times-difficult manner made him every inch his mother's son, Henry was a complex mixture of several formidable character traits.

Undeniably, Henry, like so many colourful personalities of that era, could act and act well. Upon any stage, whether majestic or otherwise, the articulate Henry could easily masquerade and perform like an intelligent and extremely talented court jester. His vast knowledge of classical phrases, idioms and humorous anecdotes, all delivered in a fluent and beautifully cultured voice, made it possible for Henry to successfully toy and play with any unwary guest or companion, whether he or she be monarch or commoner. Indeed, very few could match his incredible wit, so often deliberately tailored to suit the occasion, and cleverly disguised as exaggerated praise. Yet any yarn spun by Henry that possibly hinted towards another's failure or misfortune was always handled tactfully, given warmly and generously, and – importantly – without any trace of sarcasm. Cruel disdain assisted by self-opinionated posturing was not at all Henry's style, and, should anyone dare to contest his ability for comedy by acting tastelessly or performing in an undignified manner, the impolite perpetrator would quickly benefit from a terse verbal lashing.

Henry, though, was not deluded or paranoid over his more than evident abilities and nor did he subscribe to *trahison desclercs* (intellectual treason) by dressing down nor by initiating long hair and a dirty and unkempt beard. Furthermore, unlike a significant number of intellectuals, he did not purposely seek refuge in totally false modesty or benign humility. On the contrary, Henry was always available and ready for a demanding challenge, a fair fight, and nothing would please him more than to have a vigorous tongue-in-cheek debate, especially on the more controversial topics. Although war and conflict were issues that were strictly taboo, and therefore usually omitted from any agenda, Henry loved and often courted disagreement during these exciting *parleys*. A recent fashion that foolishly declares, and then unwisely labels, all forms of discrimination as unquestionably evil was one particular bugbear that annoyed Henry immensely. To Henry, well aware of nature's very own system of evolution that purposely and quite vigorously discriminates, those wearisome communalists who dream of a completely equal society were nothing more than ill-informed and uneducated representatives of a failed and obsolete structure of centralised government. The well-coined phrase 'champagne socialist' comes immediately to mind. He particularly loathed ideology that condemned the favouring of excellence and pigeonholed competitiveness as a category of elitism – a format that in Henry's opinion correctly encourages success and rewards good behaviour. Moreover he despised the dumbing down of learning and the practice of not allowing an advanced education for the more gifted or brighter children, regardless of their background and particularly of their parents' wealth.

To recap upon Henry's political beliefs, he was a truly caring 'One Nation' Tory, a constituent who was very much admired by his local Conservative Member of Parliament, Sir Cranley Onslow. Henry treated such disagreeable discord with utter contempt and would frequently accuse these Procrustean educational levellers of betrayal and of deliberately endorsing a contemptible programme of underhand social engineering for their own misguided political ends. More than this, Henry recognised that their wilful stupidity and their relentless drive to promote anonymous equality tended to mischievously divert apt and wicked discrimination away from its core roots – racial, religious and cultural differences. These are real and dangerous issues that, as a practising and devout Catholic, Henry truly abhorred.

In complete contrast, however, the more equal roles of the modern woman and the political question of greater European harmony were subjects that Henry simply adored, and matters upon which he welcomed an opportunity to provide an opinion. With convincing charm and a schoolboy's innocence, he enjoyed fuelling any argument by purposely playing devil's advocate, and by introducing either chauvinistic or isolationist points of view. In seeking out possible weaknesses in the judgement of others, Henry knew that retribution could possibly follow, especially from those not best pleased by his humorous and rather taunting interventions. Unperturbed and with calm composure Henry always managed to ride any storm that came his way, including any open criticism of his views regardless of whether he had delivered them with genuine sincerity or otherwise. In spite of this, the upshot of these debates had a familiar tone; not one person would have been adversely affected by an encounter with Henry and almost everyone would end up laughing.

'As you may remember my saying years ago how afraid I was of Henry when I first knew him but once I had got over that fear I grew very fond of him with his sense of humour and his teasing!'
Molly, Addlestone, Surrey

'Bless him, Henry was one of those rare individuals who always

spoke his mind, and no matter how critical he was being, you knew he was being constructive, and you respected him for it. He had such a distinctive voice which he used to good effect, particularly when greeting one in a crowded room!

'I wonder what Henry would have said about the French trawler men and their antics? I know he loved his fishing, and would have had a word or two about their methods. But he would have berated them without being malicious or be-littleing (spelling?) about it. He was unique and quite incomparable.'

Elizabeth, Woking, Surrey

'Henry was a one-off. A unique embodiment of the life force and a great contributor to the gaiety of his friends. I relished our frequent set-to's about the Poll Tax and life in general.'

Richard, Woking, Surrey

'Henry was always such fun to talk to, and so marvellously cheerful – he will be greatly missed by all his friends.'

Cranley, House of Commons

Despite these rather wilful displays of naughtiness, Henry was never more genuinely warm than when performing his role as confidant, especially when family and friends were in crisis, torn over principle or decision. Henry, at ease and in harmony with his own way of life, was ideally placed to provide advice, whether favourable or otherwise, although it was never given judgementally. That specific task would fall to others.

Although over the years there were many occasions when Henry's calm composure came to the fore, there is one particular incident that clearly helps to demonstrate his more oblique and compassionate sides. During an exceptional moment of candidness, and in spite of the event happening so many years ago, Betty's younger sister, Margaret, clearly remembers an instance where Henry showed rather old-fashioned gallantry and exemplary kindness:

'1954 was a year of immense uncertainty in my life. A very charming but much older man had proposed to me and I really didn't know what to do or to whom I could turn. I was so unsure and obviously concerned over what people may think, that Betty must have spoken to Henry. What happened then was quite extraordinary; alone and

without invitation Henry called around to see me. He didn't even tell Betty. Although his actual words are long forgotten I do remember Henry acting extremely warmly. He was very supportive and reassuring. He told me quite categorically that he had no doubts about him, believing him to be a fine and upstanding gentleman and that I should consider my well-being and happiness before worrying about what others may say. Well the rest is known, we were happily married and remained so.'

'Henry always seemed larger than life with his vitality and robustness and that wonderful laugh – it never failed to make everyone chuckle and cheer up. At a time in my life when things were very unsettled and unhappy Henry provided a haven of security – I shall always remember him with great affection and admiration.'

Cha, Tunbridge Wells, Kent

In layman's terms, these touching tributes clearly reveal that Henry Stirling was a good and kind man who refused to waste words condemning human frailties, but showed how the giving of time and gifted understanding to the concerns of others was far more beneficial. Open-minded theologians would undoubtedly describe Henry as a steadfast follower of Simon Peter, who throughout his life ministered to others, not by the preaching of deep and meaningful words but by caring and strong altruistic deeds.

Henry – alas! – was not immortal, and much to the surprise of all who knew him, he finally began to succumb to the ravages of age. Like so many of his 'live and play hard' contemporaries, Henry had unwittingly surrendered to a rather humorous, clever and extremely appropriate saying: 'Time tells on a man – especially too much of a good time!' Also very noticeable was that, although Henry was still very much in tune with life and took a lively interest in all that was going on in the world at large, his ailing heart had increasingly incapacitated him. With further surgery ruled out of the question, and without the assistance of an efficient cardiovascular system to carry oxygen and vital nutrients to all parts of his body, his physical strength was rapidly in decline.

'Henry was an example to us all how to make light of a serious health problem. He never seemed to allow it to interfere with life and was such an exhilarating companion.'

W. Hackett-Pain (Wenks), Monmouth, Gwent

'Dear Henry, he always looked so young – one could still imagine him as a Prep school boy with his lovely shock of hair. He had such a marvellous enjoyment of life which he kept to the very end.'
Margaret and Derek, Guildford, Surrey

'None of us really knew Henry was so ill as he kept his spirits up always – we shall remember Henry as always laughing and making others laugh. He gave so much of himself and was very special to us all.'
Tom and Ruth, Guildford, Surrey

Sadly, with Henry's health beginning to falter, the customary New Year's Day party that he and Betty hosted in January 1992 was the last occasion when Henry could spin his rhetorical magic. Yet in spite of his spirited attitude to a serious heart condition that had become irreconcilable to future longevity, those close to him could tell that all was not quite well. Although his laughter could still be heard above the joyous confusion, Henry had rather forlornly forgotten the wonderful times when up until recently he had gathered so many salmon and sea trout. So much more than this was that, regardless of looking at least ten years younger than his true age, Henry finally accepted that his fishing days were almost over. Be that as it may, his pragmatism remained steadfast, and Henry was most certainly not at a loss. Although solo ventures into woodlands and lakes were now destined to be fresh memories, which would join recollections of his one-time sporting prowess and the driving of his treasured Wolseley 6/99 and his much loved Range Rover, he was determined to keep busy and to continue fishing upon the lakes at Effingham. (Sadly Henry's last fishing trip was to Mallards Mere at Effingham on 11 October. Needless to say, he had success catching a large trout by way of a black-haired nymph.)[1]

As soon as it was springtime, however, Henry industriously gathered together his amazing collection of rods and reels, and in a flash he decided to sell all those that were no longer needed. He did, though, grant a reprieve to several old favourites as keepsakes. Soon after, at a family get-together where, as usual, Henry was merrily chatting away and providing much amusement, he suddenly delivered with a great fervour a quote that will always be remembered: "Convert into money, John – that's what I'll do."

Within a few weeks, an excited Henry had arranged to have a

tabletop stall at St John's Village Hall, which was situated only a few miles from his home in Woking. It was time to put his new theory into practice. As soon as family members had parked in the very convenient car park that lies adjacent, bedlam erupted. An excitable man had quickly approached his vehicle, and, before anyone could say Jack Robinson, Henry was bartering over the price of his fishing tackle. Within moments, Henry was chuckling away and was looking very smug. He had agreed upon a price and in an instant had sold the lot. Unfortunately, though, Henry's marketing skills had also somewhat faded. No longer interested in the cut and thrust of business, and believing that talk of money was generally most improper, Henry had sold at a song, making a very obvious dealer extremely happy. Nothing, however, was mentioned, and, in keeping with Henry's past zeal for the marketplace, everyone present knew that he had thoroughly enjoyed the whole affair.

Incidentally, in terms of style, particularly regarding the growth of consumerism that has swept across Western society and is currently gaining frightening proportions in Eastern Europe and China, Henry was once again something of an enigma. The vulgarity of the extremely well-off, forever striving for more, and the insensitive actions of racketeers deliberately using the distorted housing market simply to acquire for themselves even greater disposable revenue were in Henry's mind highly immoral. This was especially so if the practice was being cunningly utilised by those overpaid fat-cat professionals, who with their obscene bonus handouts unscrupulously began acquiring property in picturesque rural villages, with money laundering and eventually profit as their sole motive. Henry could tell from the increasing cost of his fishing holidays, which were becoming disproportionately more expensive every season, that this underhand investment practice would inevitably drive up house prices. This was making continuity of born-and-bred true locals actually residing in these areas in times to come, highly unlikely. In this sense, Henry, who as an environmentalist hugely enjoyed visits to the countryside, was very much a political dinosaur. He was much more in tune with the old socialist left rather than the crop of modern-day politicians from all parties, who argue quite vehemently that what they do in their private life is a matter for their own conscience and as such should be of no concern to others. This attitude, however, should not in any way be misinterpreted. Henry was not against people downsizing or buying more expensive homes in order to facilitate their own particular needs or their way of life, for he had done the very same thing. His gripe was with greedy speculators within the property market that tended to fuel the housing crisis, particularly for the young and the lower paid.

Henry always appeared content with his own good fortune, which included a generous portfolio of sound blue-chip holdings, acquired when his income had allowed it. He was not a man always seeking to gain a quick buck by gambling on the London Stock Exchange or trusting his luck at the racetrack, but he generally preferred to entrust his savings to investments that involved a lower more moderate risk.

Furthermore, in spite of his privileged upbringing he also understood alternative methods of saving, spending within his means and buying only what was required. Once again, however, this rather frugal-sounding ideal should be kept in a sensible perspective. He thoroughly enjoyed a sybaritic lifestyle of good company, excellent food and fine wine, and he was unquestionably generous both to family and friends.

Another anomaly, and somewhat surprising, was his indifference to statement-making materialism. This attitude included a complete lack of interest in the collecting of any valuable objets d'art. Accordingly, rare watercolours, oils and lavish antiques such as quality Edwardian furniture possibly inlaid with rich mahogany, or items of Victorian silver miscellanea and expensive Minton china were never purchased to adorn his unpretentious home. In fact, Moor Cottage with its numerous nooks and crannies, which experts in the field of decor and representatives of either Sotheby's or Christie's would probably argue were in dire need of ornate marble or moulded iron urns and small Regency chiffoniers graciously enhanced by bronze art nouveau, could be accurately described as being only modestly furnished. Any closer inspection would also quickly discover that, although the home was furnished extremely tastefully, most items, including pieces of quality Staffordshire and several Victorian brass carriage clocks, were invariably either second-hand purchases or inherited family keepsakes.

Henry, not content with announcing his new ideology on life, still insisted upon partying whatever the cost. Nothing would please him more than to cast his net in the direction of his old friends with an invitation to lunch. With a concept that true friends demand

'A man's a man for a' that – Robert Burns, a fellow Scot.

nothing of each other, Henry, who was no longer able to fully enjoy the gathering of game from fishing, found some compensation from gathering his companions around his table in fellowship. Whenever possible, he would willingly make headway for the kitchen and take responsibility for the cooking. Although a great lover of smoked trout and salmon, Henry also enjoyed shellfish and simply adored the wonderful aroma that came with preparing Irish soda bread and moules à la marinière. Unperturbed by those who accuse them of being dangerous to eat, and knowing that mussels are at their best in cold weather, making their season from October to March, this was just another delight that came along with the autumn bonfires. Melting the butter over a low heat before adding delicately chopped onion and a touch of garlic into the pan was a thrilling experience, of which Henry made the most. Its apogee, and the moment when Henry was at his best, was when he began to include copious amounts of good quality white wine. So great was Henry's enthusiasm that more often that not he had to be reminded to tip in the mussels as soon as the magnificent mix had come to the boil. According to the recipes of most culinary experts the dish should then be garnished with cream and the onions discarded; this, though, was not Henry's way. His garnish was lashings of freshly milled black pepper and, when available, slices of lemon. To add to the occasion, further white wine and several pints of Guinness would be shared, making the consummation of Henry's very special moules à la marinière an exquisite and cosmopolitan experience.

In spite of Henry's wide-ranging almost international background, in the popular sense he could never truly aspire to having achieved the status of being a national icon. Nevertheless, his gregarious nature together with a passion for keeping good company and sharing excellent cuisine certainly helped him on his way to becoming a highly regarded local celebrity, especially in and around Woking.

Henry's unique manner and unfailing sense of humour were two character traits that were very much admired, particularly when both were ably delivered by a natural bias in favour of a warm smile and a more than generous laugh. As well as being able to promote an uncanny flair for problem-solving, by reducing difficulties to their simplest terms and thereafter adopting uncomplicated solutions, his unquestionable charm was also capable in piloting compromise and goodwill – a quality required within any committee. These attributes and Henry's love of life are echoed by several friends and associates of the Woking Seniors Club – a vocation organisation that offers support and companionship to community members. Typically, the ageless Henry and a few of his more enlightened companions would deliberately play down the worthwhile aims of the philanthropic club, by insisting on renaming the local fellowship the Woking Seniles!

Partying whatever the cost: a smiling Henry with his hands tucked in his belt has just left the sunroom of Moor Cottage in order to receive a humorous vote of thanks from his great pal, Peter Paine (standing by Henry's side).

'I have known Henry since he joined the Seniors Club and I served on the committee with him. I am so very sorry.'
Cheslyn (Lyn) Mileham, Woking, Surrey

'Members of the Senior's Club will long remember Henry for his good company and humour and it was a pleasure and a privilege to have known him.'
Norman, Woking, Surrey

'Going to the "Seniles" with Henry was always enjoyable with his great sense of humour and memorable stories to suit every occasion.'

John Moseley, Woking, Surrey

'It will be very hard for us all to think of life without Henry. Over many years he has been one of the "solid" group whether in the garden, seniors lunches or parties, and I have so enjoyed his company and all that he stood for.'

Guy, Woking, Surrey

'We were very fond of Henry – he certainly bought a breath of fresh air and humour to Woking – especially Christmas drinks parties.'

Clare, Kennington, London

ACT II

'Happy Memories. All my love, B.
And Tight Lines.'

Betty's short farewell and cryptic message to Henry, written on the end of the card that accompanied her magnificent floral tribute.

The remaining few days of Henry Hay Dundas Stirling's time on earth were by no means sad, nor did they offer a distressing anticlimax to his wonderful life. On the contrary, Henry continued to speak at the top of his form, and would greet those that had ventured to his hospital bed in order to wish him well, with a warm smile and a cheerful tale – and, on the Friday evening prior to his passing, a drink of malt! Such was Henry's sway with life's rich pageant that it would be perfectly reasonable to suggest that, like most mortals, especially those who had long accepted their precarious position, he would perhaps readily pray for little fuss or unnecessary bother. Not Henry, however, for that was never to be Henry's style. Without a care in the world he suggested a banquet – a final party where he could sip champagne and devour smoked-salmon sandwiches made in the Irish way with soda bread. The task to arrange this feast fell to another of Henry's close friends and fishing companions, Dr Geoffrey Ambrose. Dutifully, and without questioning the true wisdom of the occasion, all was arranged, including an ice bucket. Henry could not tolerate poorly chilled champagne even if the expensive drink was to be subsequently poured into a glass containing cold Guinness.

The following morning, Saturday, 27 March 1993, after saying a cheery good morning to one of the young nurses, Henry simply closed his eyes and fell asleep for his very last time. Visitors, staff and family, however, will always be astonished by the almost eerie tranquillity that existed behind the drawn curtains that shielded his window-view bed from the rest of the rather functional cardiac ward of St Peter's Hospital. Indeed, what was particularly striking was the calm composure of Henry's face. What was perhaps more amazing was that onlookers would have certainly not known that Henry had actually died. With his naturally aristocratic air aided by a craggy chin and crop of auburn hair that remained dominant, Henry looked as though he was shrewdly taking an afternoon siesta after having toiled the morning away in his beautiful garden at Moor Cottage. He was gone and yet to the small world around him, nurses and family alike, he had displayed not only how a dignified life of *carpe diem* should be lived, but also how with equal dignity it should end.

For those who shared his unwavering faith, one other matter had clearly been resolved; Henry's soul was at eternal peace and in a status of spiritual ascendancy.

Thereafter at his much loved St Dunstan's, before a packed requiem Mass, there could not have been a more fitting tribute and celebration of Henry's wonderful life than the magnificent eulogy given by his friend Dominic O'Donnell. Yet – so typical of the mischievous Henry! – there was more to follow. Only hours later, another extremely moving incident occurred. It was an occasion that will always be remembered. As Henry's shining coffin was gently cradled and then cautiously lowered by the bearers into the open grave, several family mourners were conscious that a strong breeze had developed. It suddenly began to rustle the leaves and branches of the line of sorbus whitebeam and of the *robur* (common) oaks, which stand like papal Swiss guards protecting the Catholic left side of Send Cemetery. It was as if they too could recognise that a close and dear friend had been lost and in their own very special way they were waving their goodbyes.

'Life will never be the same without Henry. I have never known anyone like him – there can't be anyone else like him I'm certain. I shall miss him so much.'

Eunice, Upper Easebourne, West Sussex

'Of course we shall all miss Henry, who enjoyed life, and managed to inspire others to do the same.'

Peggy and Donald Pickett, Woking, Surrey

'Henry was a wonderful man who faced up to life and all it had to offer with great spirit, and always had a twinkle in his eye. We have many happy memories of him.'

Johnny and Rosie, Topsham, Devon

'Henry fought a long battle with ill-health, and I always admired him for his courage and cheerfulness. Speed you well, Henry! I will so much miss Henry, and that windy corner by the Oriental Stores where we used to stand and chat. Matters will never be the same again.'

Tony, Woking, Surrey

'I so enjoyed Henry's sense of humour, and I shall miss his cheerful banter when I am next shopping in Waitrose!'

Joan de Jonge, West Byfleet, Surrey

'I know Shirley has written for us both, but I did very much want to write you a note. Henry's kindness in being willing and able to help others was legendary.'

Graham, Woking, Surrey

'Although Susan only met Henry once she has often said that she thought he was the nicest gentleman she has ever met. We return to England in June to live near Winchester and hope we will see you at my mother's sometime in the near future.'

Robert and Susan, London, Ontario, Canada

'As you know I have been looking after Henry for a while and

latterly he was suffering from increasingly severe heart failure. In spite of this very significant illness he remained cheerful and was an inspiration to us all.'

Michael Joy, MD, FRCP, FACC, FESC, FRAeS,
Longcross, Surrey

Within a recent biographical study of the illustrious Sir Winston Leonard Spencer Churchill, Richard Holmes, Professor of Military and Security Studies at Cranfield University and the Royal Military College of Science, quotes Sir George Mallaby, Cabinet Office Undersecretary during the Second World War. The following passage comes from a much larger article. The former high commissioner to New Zealand describes the courageous war leader as "unusual, unpredictable, exciting, original, stimulating, provocative, humorous, entertaining – almost everything a man could be, a great man!"[2]

Without question, each and every one of these fine epithets could also portray the many qualities of Henry. And perhaps even more fundamental, and somewhat cloaked by the enormity of phrases and quotations, is the extremely poignant saying that 'Men who have enjoyed life seldom fear death'.

Henry Hay Dundas Stirling, who was indeed fortunate to live throughout Britain's finest period of the twentieth century – the Golden Age – and who passionately enjoyed a way of living which was totally immersed in a gregarious melting pot of *Fun, Flies and Laughter*, was unquestionably such a man.

Eulogy

HENRY STIRLING
(1919 – 1993)

'Do not go gentle into that good night,
Old age should burn and rave at close of day;
Rage, rage against the dying of the light.'

from *Do Not Go Gentle into That Good Night* by Dylan Thomas

Henry Stirling was born in 1919, the son of a Scottish father and an Irish mother. He spent his childhood in British India, and this privileged start may have given him that taste for the good things in life, which lasted till the end of his days. After Downside, he went to Cambridge but, being impatient to get into the war, he volunteered for the army without completing his course. He and Betty married in 1941 and he was posted to the Middle East the same year, so their relationship began with four years' separation.

Henry was severely wounded in Egypt and spent a year in hospital in Cairo. He was whisked off to Kashmir by his mother, who had friends in high places, and spent the rest of the war convalescing and fishing there, much to the chagrin of his lonely bride in London. Returning to England in 1945, with no prospects of a job and no degree, he resumed his studies, this time at Oxford. He graduated in forestry and then made a career in the fruit-importing trade, staying with one company and rising to board level before illness forced his early retirement in 1977.

Since then he has courageously fought his heart condition. There have been any number of alarms and spells in intensive care, and other illnesses. Until this his last bout, which he lost, he always seemed a great survivor, emerging from treatment with an undiminished appetite for life and with his natural buoyancy of spirit unimpaired.

Henry was a fisherman, like the disciples by the Sea of Galilee. They were professionals; he an enthusiastic amateur. But he was a disciple too, a man of deep religious faith and conviction. He bore his Christian witness not by preaching, as they did, but by example. This parish has lost a most dutiful and devoted son.

And Woking has lost a great character. Encounters with Henry were never dull. In many ways his personality was as elusive, slippery and changeable as the fish he loved to pursue. He was more than direct. He could be loud, sharp and outrageous. But, whatever he said, it was difficult to be angry with him for long. Underneath the belligerence, the mischief and the provocation there was no malice, but a kind, shy, sensitive man, muddying the waters a little so that he could slip away. It was a defensive manoeuvre to protect himself from the world.

Henry was able to relate to people of all classes. When at home he was quiet and withdrawn for much of the time, but company brought out the best in him. He was a collector of characters and rejoiced in the richness and variety of human foibles. Most of his stories were about the quirkiness of others. He was full of enthusiasms and eager to communicate these – for fish, of course, for good food, his potent home-brewed beer, his garden, his friends. He relished all these things, and especially parties, conviviality and laughter. The memory of his penetrating laugh rising over the hubbub of a crowd will stay with us all for many years. He liked and respected women, treating them as worthy sparring partners on occasion, but usually with great courtesy and charm. He was a maverick in many of his opinions – a Conservative who was agin the government, an unpredictable, an original, a bit of a rebel. Perhaps that was the Irish in him.

Of the years he spent in business I can say nothing; but an old colleague wrote to Betty saying that Henry was 'like a gale of fresh air' in the office. He was a romantic and loved the Central London markets where he worked for their chaos, congestion and humanity. He was sad to see them dispersed.

Henry was blessed with youthful looks. There was a bloom about him, boyishness, and that enviable head of auburn hair that hardly faded. He was like a tree; he had presence and stature, a deeply rooted faith, an earthiness in his character, and, that rare virtue, stability – one job all his life, many years in the same house, one family, one best friend and companion, Betty.

"Carpe diem!" he said to me on his doorstep only a few weeks ago – then, severely, "You know what it means? – Live for today. Don't put off meeting your friends; make the most of what time you have." Henry certainly set us an example in that.

Last year, despite ailing health, he went fishing in an open boat off the coast of Mayo, and came home half frozen, to be thawed out with duvets and whisky. Then last December he found it was possible to buy a barrel of oysters in Woking and he hosted an oyster feast for some of his friends, attending to every detail of the table himself.

In his last week at St Peter's, as well as receiving the sacrament of the sick, he asked Betty for a smoked salmon sandwich, made in the Irish way, with finely chopped onions and some capers. Even at the end he wanted life to be a party. And he went home in style.

It has been a privilege to know him. Age could not wither him nor custom stale his infinite variety. May he rest in peace.

Dominic McDonnell

The Life and Times of
Henry Hay Dundas Stirling

1919 *Born in Simla, British Imperial India on 3 July.* First trans-Atlantic flight.

1920 League of Nations created. Government of Ireland Act partitioned Ireland.

1922 Continuing civil war in Ireland.

1924 First Labour government in Britain, under Ramsay MacDonald, replaced by the Conservative Unionists under Stanley Baldwin. Death of Lenin.

1928 Women over twenty-one given the vote. GEC develop the first television images.

1929 Wall Street Crash and world economic depression.

1930 World record cricket innings by Don Bradman: 452 not out during a match between Queensland and New South Wales.

1933 *Entered Downside School.* Adolf Hitler became Chancellor of Germany.

1936 Death of George V. Edward VIII became King yet abdicated in favour of his brother George VI – the Mrs Wallis Simpson affair.

1938 *Entered Peterhouse College Cambridge reading mechanical engineering.* On 3 July Gresley's Class A4 Pacific steam locomotive *Mallard* attained the world speed record of 126 mph.

1939 On September 3 Britain declared war on Germany. *On September 26 the Cambridge University Joint Recruitment Board recommended that volunteer Henry be trained as an officer in the Royal Artillery.*

1940 Netherlands surrendered to German forces. Belgium capitulated. Italy entered the war. France was defeated and signed armistice with Germany. Blitz on London begins on 7 September.

1941 *Granted Commission to 2nd Lieutenant Royal Artillery on 21 March. Married Betty Hawley at St Philip's Catholic Church, Finchley, North London on 3 May. Embarked for Egypt on 20 September. Wounded in Libya in November.* Germany invaded USSR. Pacific War began with the attack on the US fleet at Pearl Harbor on 7 December.

1942 Montgomery was made commander of British 8th Army. Field Marshal Erwin Rommel, the Desert Fox, stared at defeat. British retook Tobruk.

1942/3 *Meanwhile Henry was fishing and shooting in the Kashmir.*

1943 Mussolini resigned. German forces occupied Rome. British midget submarines attacked German battleship *Tirpitz*. Italy declared war on Germany

1944 *Classified as unfit for military service on 15 November.* Allies landed in Normandy (Operation Overlord). First V-1 flying bomb fell on England. First V-2 rocket fell on England.

1945 On 27 March, last V-2 rocket fell on England. In April Mussolini was executed by partisans. Hitler committed suicide. 8 May VE day. On 6 and 8 August atomic bombs were dropped on Hiroshima and Nagasaki leading to the Japanese surrender. Labour Party under Clement Atlee won the general election, replacing the wartime leader Winston Churchill. The American journalist Walter Lippmann described superpower confrontation as the 'Cold War'. Churchill on a similar theme uttered the phrase 'Iron Curtain'. *Henry returned to London.*

1946 *First child, Jennifer Deirdre, was born. Henry matriculated at St Catherine's University, Oxford.* First meeting of the General Assembly of the United Nations.

1947 The London Midland and Scottish became the first railway to operate diesel-electric locomotives on main lines. India partitioned.

1948 *Second child, David Anselan James Dundas, was born.* Mohandas Gandhi assassinated. Establishment of the State of Israel. First Arab-Israeli war. British National Health Service founded. Britain developed the first storage computer.

1949 *Awarded honours degree in forestry.* NATO formed. Soviet Union detonated first nuclear bomb. Communist victory in China. Comedian Tommy Handley famous for weekly programme *ITMA* died.

1950 *Commenced work with the Deciduous Fruit Board.*
1950/3 Korean War.
1952   George VI died. Elizabeth II became Queen. First jet airliner built – the British Comet. General Dwight D. Eisenhower, Allied Supreme Commander North-West Europe during 1944/5, was elected US President.
1953   The coronation of Her Majesty Queen Elizabeth II took place. Sir Edmund Hillary and Sherpa Tenzing reached the summit of Mount Everest.
1954   Roger Bannister became the first man to break the four-minute mile (3 minutes 59.4 seconds).
1956   *Third child, Fiona Jane, born. 'Beats the Panel' on* **What's My Line?** Suez crisis occurred. Second Arab-Israeli war. Elvis Presley entered the UK Charts with 'Heartbreak Hotel'. Jim Laker took 19 for 90, to rout the Australians as England retained the Ashes.
1957   De Gaulle became leader of the Fifth Republic of France. Treaty of Rome established the EEC.
1958   *The Stirlings move to Moor Cottage, Woking, and Henry joined the local Conservatives.*
1959   The Vietnam War began. 'Living Doll' entered UK Charts. Cliff Richard was nominated by the *New Musical Express* as the best newcomer to the pop scene.
1960   John F. Kennedy was elected US President. Gary Powers was shot down over Russia.
1961   The Berlin Wall was built. Yuri Gagarin in *Vostok 1* became the first man in space. US-backed Cuban rebels were repulsed at the Bay of Pigs. The Beatles made their Cavern Club debut. Within two years they would top the UK charts.
1962   The Cuban Missile Crisis occurred. Cricket's Gentlemen v Players came to an end after more than 150 years.
1963   President Kennedy was assassinated. The Profumo Affair weakened Macmillan's government. Martin Luther King proclaimed "I have a dream."
1964   The PLO (Palestine Liberation Organisation) was established. In Cyprus violence erupted between Turkish and Greek communities. Nelson Mandela was sentenced to life imprisonment. Bob Dylan entered the UK charts with the protest song, 'The Times They Are A-Changin' '. Freddie Truman (Yorkshire and Derbyshire) became the first cricketer to take 300 wickets in test cricket – when asked if anyone would beat his achievement, he replied, "Aye, but whoever does will be bloody tired." Muhammad Ali, formerly

Cassius Clay, won the world heavyweight title, and proclaimed, "When you're as great as I am it is hard to be humble!"

1965 Rhodesia declared UDI (Unilateral Declaration of Independence). War between India and Pakistan.

1966 England won the football World Cup beating West Germany 4–2.

1967 Third Arab-Israeli war (Six Day War). Sandi Shaw won the Eurovision Song Contest with 'Puppet on a String'.

1968 Martin Luther King and Senator Robert Kennedy were assassinated. The great West Indian cricketer, Sir Garfield Sobers, hit Malcolm Nash, the Glamorgan bowler, for six sixes in an over.

1969 The United States put men on the moon. The IRA commenced their campaign of terror. Supersonic Concorde's first flight took place.

1971 War between India and Pakistan led to the creation of Bangladesh. The Goon, author and comedian Spike Milligan – best known for his dying words: "I told you I was ill" – wrote his bestseller: *Adolf Hitler – My Part in His Downfall*.

1972 US President Nixon visited China.

1973 *Suffered from his first cardiac arrest.* Britain joined EEC. Fourth Arab-Israeli war. US withdrew from Vietnam.

1974 Bloody Sunday shootings occured in Londonderry. Nixon resigned after the Watergate scandal. Sir (James) Harold Wilson led Labour back into power.

1975 The death of General Franco led to the restoration of democracy in Spain. Margaret Thatcher became the first woman party leader in British politics.

1977 *Early retirement due to constant cardiac problems.*

1979 The Soviet Union invaded Afghanistan – they would remain there for ten years.

1980 African majority rule in Zimbabwe under Mugabe.

1981 Ronald Reagan was elected US President. Pope John Paul II survived an assassination attempt. The Space Shuttle made its maiden voyage.

1982 Falklands war with Argentina.

1984 South African government declared a state of emergency after widespread resistance to apartheid legislation. The comedians Eric Morecambe and Tommy Cooper died – Just like that! Tommy died whist performing at Her Majesty's Theatre, London.

1985 Osama bin Laden established al-Qaeda.

1986 The Chernobyl nuclear accident occurred. All seven crew of the Space Shuttle were killed as *Challenger* exploded shortly after take-off.

1989 The collapse of communism in Eastern Europe.

1990 Germany was reunified. Iraq invaded Kuwait. Margaret Thatcher resigned as Prime Minister – Thatcherism waned and John Major replaced her. Nelson Mandela was released from prison.

1991 The Maastricht Treaty was signed. ***Henry resigned from the Conservative Party***. UN Coalition forces defeated Iraq and liberated Kuwait. Collapse of USSR – Cold War ended. Introduction of the Internet.

1992 Civil war erupted in the former Yugoslavia. The Rio de Janeiro Earth Summit took place.

1993 *Henry Hay Dundas Stirling bade his farewells during the morning of Saturday, 27 March.*

Glossary for Beginners

Keen young fisherman to older friend: *"I went on a fishing trip last week and only managed to catch one blooming fish. That means that that one fish cost me six hundred blooming pounds."*

Older friend's retort: *"Look at it this way, if it was that blooming much for one, it's blooming lucky that you didn't catch two!"*

Barb	A jagged piece on the hook of the fly.
Beat	A fishing lake or river is very often divided into stretches of bank that are called beats.
Butt	Handle of fly-rod.
Cast	The nylon link between line and fly.
Casting	The art form of using a rod to propel line, leader and fly across the water and over any fish.
Close Season	Prescriptive periods during the year when rivers and other designated beats are not fished in order to allow spawning.
Figure-of-Eight Knot	A knot used to join the line to lead.
Fly	The feathered hook to attract and catch fish. Henry's favourite flies: black spider, buzzers (various sizes including green-ribbed), pellet, shrimp and silver-bodied black-haired! Nymph flies: black-haired, damsel, green, hare's-ear, olive, orange, pheasant-tail and pink.
Fly-Box	A box in which you keep your treasured flies.

Fly-Tying	The art form of making a fly.
Fly-Holder	The circle of wire above the rod butts to which flies are attached. This stops flies flailing about when rods are being used.
Foul-Hook	To hook a fish somewhere other than in its mouth.
Half-Blood Knot	Common knot made to join fly to leader.
Hook	Can be single, double or treble.
Hooked	Hooking a fish.
Kill	Catching, landing and killing the fish.
Land	The art of bringing a fish to the bank or into a catch net.
Leader	The nylon link between line and fly.
Net	A flexible creel made from steel rings and strong netting, which is used to bring the catch to the bank.
Nylon	The link between line and fly, also called a cast or leader.
Play	The art form (struggle) that immediately occurs between the angler and the fish once it has been hooked.
Pull	The moment a fish takes the fly and thereafter rejects it.
Reel	A cylinder on which the fishing line may be wound.
Rings	The wire loops or guides on the fishing rod through which the line is threaded.
Rising	Fish that rise above the waterline searching for food.
Rod	The long slender pole carrying a fishing line.
Sinking Line	The method of sinking the line in order to take the fly down towards the fish – a cold-weather or high-water ploy that is particularly effective.
Tackle	Fishing equipment.
Touch	The moment a fish touches the fly.
Waders	Extended rubber wellingtons that enable the wearer to wade either up to the thigh or chest.

Appendix

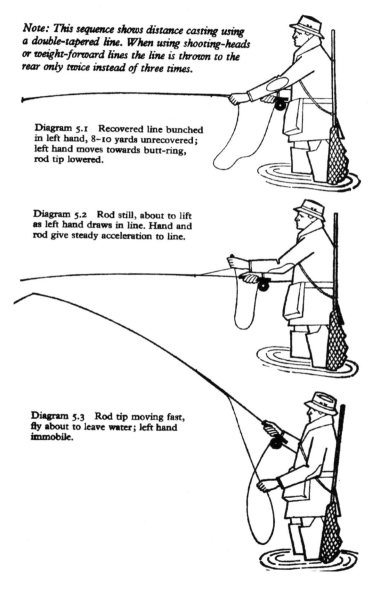

Note: This sequence shows distance casting using a double-tapered line. When using shooting-heads or weight-forward lines the line is thrown to the rear only twice instead of three times.

Diagram 5.1   Recovered line bunched in left hand, 8–10 yards unrecovered; left hand moves towards butt-ring, rod tip lowered.

Diagram 5.2   Rod still, about to lift as left hand draws in line. Hand and rod give steady acceleration to line.

Diagram 5.3   Rod tip moving fast, fly about to leave water; left hand immobile.

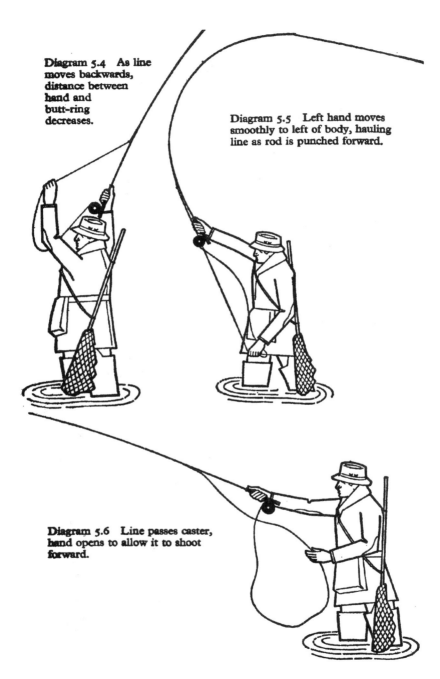

Diagram 5.4 As line moves backwards, distance between hand and butt-ring decreases.

Diagram 5.5 Left hand moves smoothly to left of body, hauling line as rod is punched forward.

Diagram 5.6 Line passes caster, hand opens to allow it to shoot forward.

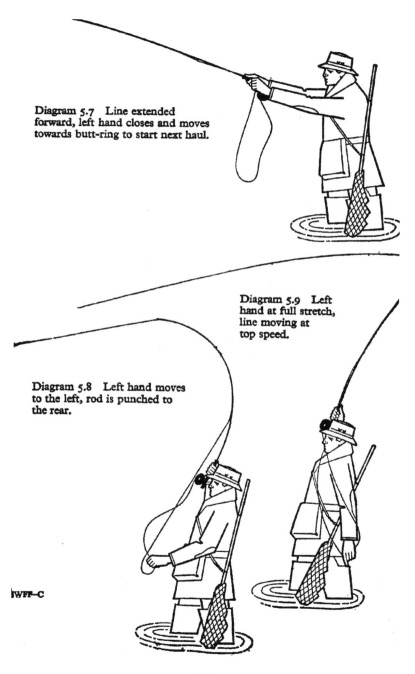

Diagram 5.7 Line extended forward, left hand closes and moves towards butt-ring to start next haul.

Diagram 5.9 Left hand at full stretch, line moving at top speed.

Diagram 5.8 Left hand moves to the left, rod is punched to the rear.

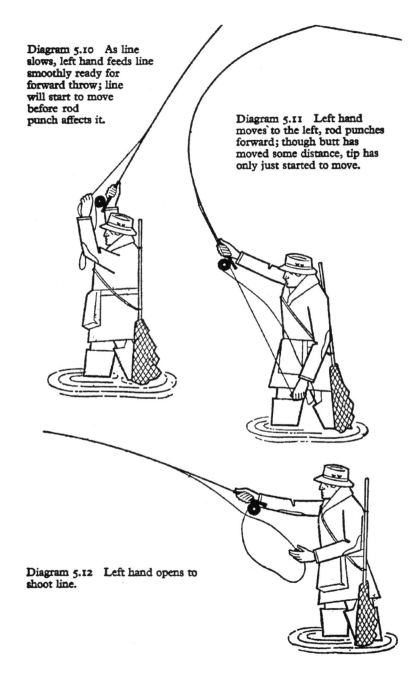

Diagram 5.10 As line slows, left hand feeds line smoothly ready for forward throw; line will start to move before rod punch affects it.

Diagram 5.11 Left hand moves to the left, rod punches forward; though butt has moved some distance, tip has only just started to move.

Diagram 5.12 Left hand opens to shoot line.

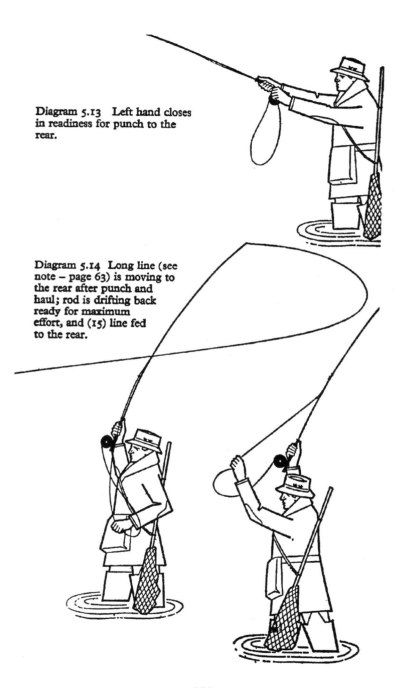

Diagram 5.13 Left hand closes in readiness for punch to the rear.

Diagram 5.14 Long line (see note – page 63) is moving to the rear after punch and haul; rod is drifting back ready for maximum effort, and (15) line fed to the rear.

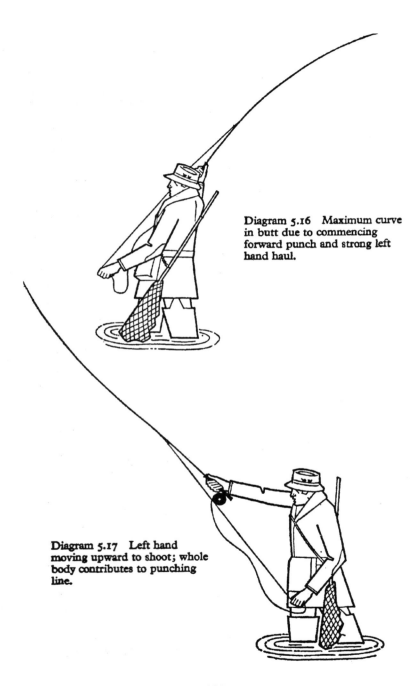

Diagram 5.16 Maximum curve in butt due to commencing forward punch and strong left hand haul.

Diagram 5.17 Left hand moving upward to shoot; whole body contributes to punching line.

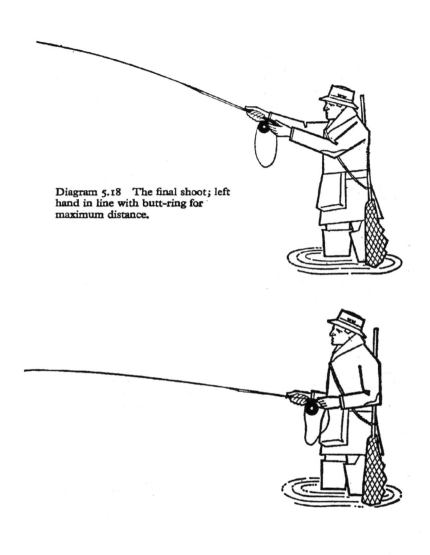

Diagram 5.18 The final shoot; left
hand in line with butt-ring for
maximum distance.

Diagram 5.19 Rod at correct fishing angle, line being recovered
by left hand.

Diagram 5.20 Taking line to commence recovery.

Diagram 5.21 Finger closes over line; thumb and forefinger grip line at X.

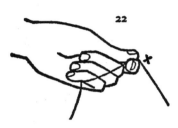

Diagram 5.22 Forefinger and thumb lifted to draw line.

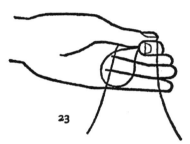

Diagram 5.23 Second, third and fourth fingers withdraw from loop and pass round it. The whole routine is then repeated.

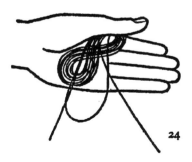

Diagram 5.24 The final result; a 'figure-of-eight' bunch.

Bibliography

Abram, D., Edwards, N., Ford, M., Sen, D., Wooldridge, B., Jacobs, D., Goodman, J., Mulchandani, A., Stone, L., and Sylge, C., *The Rough Guide to India, sixth edition*: Rough Guides, 1982.

Bain, Robert, *The Clans and Tartans of Scotland*, London and Glasgow: Collins 1947.

Bhasin, Raaja, *Viceregal Lodge and the Indian Institute of Advanced Studies, Shimla*, New Delhi: Published by the Institute's deputy secretary, 2005.

Boehm, K., and Lees-Spalding, J., *2005 Guide to Independent Schools*, Richmond, London: Trotman and Co. Ltd., 2004.

Botha, S., *Paarl Valley*, Pretoria: Human Science Research Council, 1987.

Brett, M., Johnson-Barker, B., and Renssen, M., *South Africa: Eyewitness Travel Guide, 1999*, London: Dorling Kindersley, 1999.

Brownlee, Cecily, *All at Sea – with Union-Castle*, Cape Town: Brownlee, 2000.

Buck, Edward J., CBE, *Simla Past and Present*, Shimla, India: Minerva House Publishers, 2005.

Campbell, Christy, *The World War II Fact Book, 1939–1945*, London: Macdonald & Co. (Publishers), 1985.

Chant, Chris, *Aircraft of World War II: 300 of the World's Greatest Aircraft*, London: Amber Books Ltd., 2001.

Clarke, M., *Clansman, the B & C Group Magazine, No. 35*, London: Cayzer, Irvine & Co. Ltd., 1976.

Damant, Henry, *Every Thursday at Four O'clock – Union-Castle: The Big Ship Way to South Africa,* Johannesburg: Friends of the Springbok & Lions, 1977.

Dewar, Peter Beauclerk, *Burke's Landed Gentry – Stirling Of*

Gargunnock, Scotland: 2001.

Fraser, David, *And We Shall Shock Them: The British Army in the Second World War*, London: Hodder and Stoughton, 1983.

Gove, Michael, *Michael Portillo: The Future of the Right*, London: Fourth Estate Ltd., 1995.

Hammond, Reginald J. W., *Complete Guide to Scotland*, London: Ward, Lock and Co. Ltd., 1964.

Holmes, Richard, *In the Footsteps of Churchill*, London: BBC Books, 2005.

Ivens, T. C., *Still Water Fly-Fishing*, London: Pan Books Ltd., 1970.

McNie, Alan, *Your Clan Heritage – Clan Buchanan*, Jedburgh, Scotland: Cascade Publishing Company, 1988.

Neillands, Robin, *A Fighting Retreat: Military Companies in the British Empire, 1947–97*, London: Hodder and Stoughton, 1996.

Palin, Michael, *Himalaya*, London: Weidenfeld & Nicolson, The Orion Publishing Group, 2004.

Paxman, Jeremy, *The English: A Portrait of a People*, London: Penguin Books, 1998. *The Political Animal: An Anatomy*, London: Penguin Books, 2002.

Pike, E. Royston, *Britain's Prime Ministers from Walpole to Wilson*, London: Odhams Books for The Hamlyn Publishing Group Ltd., 1968.

Endnotes and References

All quotations in the text that do not carry a footnote are either extracts from a collection of personal letters so meticulously retained by Betty Stirling or are based upon the author's interviews with individuals previously mentioned within the Acknowledgements.

CHAPTER ONE: *Pruning the Family Tree*

ACT I

1. Jeremy Paxman, *The English: A Portrait of a People*, p. 264.
2. Ibid. p. 264.
3. Alan McNie, *Your Clan Heritage – Clan Buchanan*, p. 10.
4. Robert Bain, *The Clans and Tartans of Scotland*, p. 6.
5. Ibid. p. 33.
6. Reginald J. W. Hammond, *Complete Guide to Scotland*, p. 260.
7. Ibid. p. 262.
8. Ibid. p. 262.

ACT II

9. Peter Beauclerk Dewar, *Burke's Landed Gentry – Stirling of Gargunnock.*
10. Rev. James Laurie, *Parish of Gargunnock, Presbytery of Stirling, Synod of Perth and Stirling*, p. 1.
11. Edward J. Buck, CBE, *Simla Past and Present*, p. 18.
12. Michael Palin, *Himalaya*, p. 71.
13. Raaja Bhasin, *Viceregal Lodge and the Indian Institute of Advanced Studies, Shimla*, p. 8.
14. D. Abram, N. Edwards, M. Ford, D. Sen, B. Wooldridge, D. Jacobs, J. Goodman, A. Mulchandani, L. Stone and C. Sylge. *The Rough Guide to India, sixth edition*, p. 490.
15. Ibid. p. 491.
16. Raaja Bhasin, *Viceregal Lodge and the Indian Institute of Advanced Studies, Shimla*, p. 22.
17. Ecclesiastical Records (Baptism Register), Church of St Michael and St Joseph, Shimla, dated 20 July 1919.

CHAPTER TWO: *Downside and Peterhouse*

ACT I

1. K. Boehm and J. Lees-Spalding, *2005 Guide to Independent Schools*, p. 285.
2. Ibid. p. 286.

ACT II

3. Dr P. Pattenden, Senior Tutor and Evelyn Ansell, M A, *Admissions Register, Peterhouse in the University of Cambridge, January 1931–December 1950*, p. 130.
4. Peterhouse Cambridge, www.pet.cam.ac.uk/, *Welcome to Peterhouse*, p. 1 of 1.
5. Michael Gove, *Michael Portillo: The Future of the Right*, p. 40.
6. Robin Neillands, *A Fighting Retreat: Military Companies in the British Empire, 1947-97*, p. 38.
7. Jeremy Paxman, *The Political Animal: An Anatomy*, p. 165.

CHAPTER THREE: *War, Wife and Wounded*

ACT I

1. Linda Nelson, Administration Officer, *Civil Secretariat, Historical Disclosures*, Army Personnel Centre, Glasgow. D/APC/HD/ABLV/57707.
2. Ibid.
3. Ibid.
4. Ibid.

ACT II

5. Christy Campbell, *The World War II Fact Book, 1939–1945*, p. 204.

ACT III

6. A newspaper cutting, *source unknown.*
7. Main source, Christy Campbell, *The World War II Fact Book, 1939–1945*, p. 64.
8. A newspaper cutting, *source unknown.*
9. Peter Beauclerk Dewar, *Burke's Landed Gentry – Stirling of Gargunnock.*
10. Ibid.

CHAPTER FOUR: *Safe and Home Alone*

ACT I

1. T. C. Ivens, *Still Water Fly-Fishing*, pp. 63 to 70.

ACT II

2. A commemorative programme, *A Service of Thanksgiving for the Life and Work of John Snagge, OBE, 1904–1996,* dated Wednesday, 15 May, 1996.
3. Christy Campbell, *The World War II Fact Book, 1939–1945*, p. 328.

CHAPTER FIVE: *In the Pink – Out of the Blue!*

ACT I

1. Margaret Davies, college archivist, *St Catherine's College*, Oxford.
2. www.stcatz.ox.ac.uk, dated 2 September 2005.

ACT II

3. Margaret Davies, college archivist, *St Catherine's College*, Oxford.
4. Ibid.
5. www.stcatz.ox.ac.uk, dated 2 September 2005.
6. Margaret Davies, college archivist, *St Catherine's College*, Oxford.
7. Ibid.

ACT III

8. A newspaper cutting, *source unknown, Obituary – Dr Michael Raymond.*

CHAPTER SIX: *The Peach-Tasting Marketing Detective!*

ACT I

1. M. Brett, B. Johnson-Barker and M. Renssen, *South Africa: Eyewitness Travel Guide, 1999*, pp. 60, 61, 71, 92, 138, Cape and Environs map.
2. S. Botha, *Paarl Valley*. pp. 90. 92.
3. Henry Damant, *Every Thursday at four o'clock – Union-Castle: The Big Ship Way to South Africa,* p. 9.
4. Cecily Brownlee, *All at Sea – with Union-Castle*, pp. 87, 88, 89.
5. S. Botha, *Paarl Valley*, p. 93.
6. Marcus Clarke, Editorial Consultant, *Clansman, the B & C Group Magazine, No. 35 (*formerly the *British & Commonwealth Review)*, p. 4.
7. Cecily Brownlee, *All at Sea – with Union-Castle*, pp. 93, 94, 95.
8. Ibid, p. 83.

ACT II

9. Chairman, Producer and Panel, *What's My Line?* dated 6 February 1956, BBC Television, Diploma Parchment.
10. Gilbert Harding, *letter,* dated 13 February 1956.

ACT III

11. news.bbc.co.uk, *Veteran BBC Playwright Dies,* dated 2 September 2005, p. 1 of 2.

CHAPTER SEVEN: *Parties, Fishing and Bonfires*

ACT I

1. Moldram, Clarke & Edgley. *Ref. M3/11/58. Structural Survey Report in respect of Moor Cottage, 72 Park Road, Woking,* inspected 14/11/1958.
2. E. Royston Pike, *Britain's Prime Ministers from Walpole to Wilson,* pp. 456, 457.

ACT II

3. Chris Chant, *Aircraft of World War II: 300 of the World's Greatest Aircraft,* p. 70.
4. The Western Regional Fisheries Board. *Bord Iascaigh Reigiunach an Iarthair, www.wrfb.ie/gameangling,* dated 30 October 2005, pp. 1 to 3.
5. Ibid, p. 1 to 3.
6. Ibid, p. 1 to 3.

ACT III

7. Michael Gove, *Michael Portillo: The Future of the Right,* p. 318.

CHAPTER EIGHT: *In the Footsteps of Simon*

ACT 1

1. H. H. D. Stirling, *Fishing Diary* for period 11 August 1986 until 10 October 1992, p. 70.

ACT II

2. Richard Holmes, *In the Footsteps of Churchill*, p. 295.